FARTHER ALONG

Farther Along

The Writing Journey of Thirteen Bereaved Mothers

Carol Henderson

WILLOWDELL BOOKS
CHAPEL HILL

Willowdell Books
804 Woodland Avenue
Chapel Hill, NC 27516

First Edition

Cover design and book layout by Kevin Morgan Watson

Cover photo copyright © 2012 by Kay Windsor

Lyrics to the hymn "Farther Along," appearing on page vii,
written in 1911 by Rev. W. A. Fletcher

Printed on acid-free paper
ISBN 978-1-935708-59-9

For our children

"Farther Along" is the name of a hymn, written in 1911 by an itinerant preacher named Rev. W. A. Fletcher. In 1987, Dolly Parton, Linda Ronstadt and Emmylou Harris recorded an arrangement by John Starling for their album *Trio*. It's one of our group's favorite songs.

FARTHER ALONG

Tempted and tried, we're oft made to wonder
Why it should be thus all the day long
While there are others living about us
Never molested though in the wrong

Farther along we'll know all about it
Farther along we'll understand why
Cheer up my brother, live in the sunshine
We'll understand it
all by and by

When death has come and taken our loved ones
It leaves our home so lonely and drear
Then do we wonder why others prosper
Living so wicked year after year.

Farther along . . .

Faithful 'til death, said our loving Master
A few more days to labor and wait
Toils of the road will then seem as nothing
As we sweep through the beautiful gates.

Farther along . . .

Long Afterward, I Came Upon It Again

Long afterward, I came upon it again.
I found it by accident one day,
    had assumed it was gone forever.

Yet there it was in clear view—
    like it had been waiting to be found all along.

I distinctly recall the day—
    slept later than usual,
    swigged an extra cup of coffee,
    bought oysters from a seafood stand,
    prepared to face another quiet evening.

Unexpectedly, it caught my eye—there
in the sun, blown by the wind, resting on the horizon,
    my desire to live again.

—by Barbara Goldsmith, a member of the writing group, in response
    to the prompt: "Long afterward, I came upon it again. . ."

CONTENTS

BEACH BREAK

Once I had everything I wanted; now I have everything that happened.
                                    —Peggy Clover, a member of the writing group

Recently I returned from leading a September writing retreat on a beach called Emerald Isle, off the North Carolina coast. Sounds idyllic, doesn't it? Imagine lying on the warm sand, letting your words skip across your journal page like waves curling down the beach. There you are, swimming in the bubbly surf, taking long, luxurious strolls, as pelicans swoop above the glittery water. You sit in a circle with others, sharing your newly-minted words. A salty breeze wafts off the Intracoastal Waterway. The perfect weekend.

Yes.

And no.

Yes, the weekend was luminous. But every one of us there would have given plenty *not* to qualify for membership in this elite writing retreat. If a palm reader had wandered down the beach and studied all of our hands, I bet she would have seen deep gashes across our love lines. You see, we are all bereaved mothers. We have endured what no parent can bear to even contemplate: losing a child.

"Anything but that, *please*," parents beg. "Take *my* life, not my child's."

Most of us on that weekend would probably have considered Faustian deals with the devil to get our children back. We contain within us a bottomless well of loss. But over the past decade, we've

1

proven—sometimes achingly, sometimes wondrously—that the process of putting our deepest and most hidden thoughts on the page and sharing them has helped us cope with what we all know is a lifelong struggle.

We first met in 2002 when I gave a writing workshop for bereaved mothers. "The Healing Power of the Written Word" was offered through the generosity of a hospice, a Moravian church, and a college in Winston-Salem, North Carolina. The all-day Saturday event was open to any mother who had experienced the death of a child. Women came from all over the state and even Virginia. Some, like me, had lost infants; others adult children; still others teenagers. Our children had died of illness, slowly or quickly, by accident, or suicide.

Many in this group did not consider themselves writers but were drawn to the idea of using writing to give voice to their gargantuan grief. One woman told me her need for expression was so acute that she would try most anything, "as long as it was legal."

I felt prepared for the day if a bit jittery. At the time, I taught journal writing, wrote for magazines, was the program director of a statewide writing organization, and the year before had published a memoir about my son's brief life and the ragged shadows his death had flung over my world. A mentor had encouraged me to enroll in the "Transformative Language Arts" Master's program at Goddard College in Vermont. My faculty adviser, a psychologist, and a trauma therapist had helped me plan the workshop. Still, this terrain was awesome, and I mean that in the original, thunderous, sense of the word.

There were thirteen women that first day; twelve have remained. We meet twice a year, for a weekend. Writer and teacher Roger Rosenblatt says, "Twelve is a very good number for a writing class, as it is for juries and apostles." I agree. Even though, as both leader and participant, I make us thirteen, a baker's dozen.

In our early meetings, I only occasionally shared the writings I produced in our sessions. The group had read my book and was familiar with my grief story. They needed a leader who knew, first hand, what they were experiencing but who didn't have the same urge to share. Let's just say there was abundant material in the room already, a tsunami's worth. Over time, as our prompts broadened and everyone became more relaxed, I became a more frequent contributor.

Since that first meeting we've written about our own childhoods and sibling relationships, about being schoolgirls and daughters; we've penned fiction and poetry. We've written about happy family gatherings and about trying to manage a noisy bunch of skinned-kneed children while feeling skewered inside by that always-empty seat at the kitchen table.

It is through writing, and then sharing our written words, that our group has deepened, immeasurably. I have also visited most of the women at home, going with them to accident sites, hospital corridors, and graveyards. We've sat quietly together in shut-off bedrooms. I've had the privilege of getting to know their children through reading their memory books and standing among the pictures and mementos in cherished hallway shrines. Some of those experiences have made their way into these pages.

I want you to get to know these remarkable women. They are playful and smart, incredibly courageous, and unyieldingly sad. *Farther Along* chronicles the development of our group in what reminds me of a crazy quilt. Unlike standard patchwork designs that set the pieces of fabric into a predetermined and regular grid, "crazy" quilts use ungainly swatches that produce haphazard, asymmetrical forms. In this book, big hunks of story rise up, sometimes where you'd least expect them, the way grief does.

Writing about deep and traumatic matters, as many studies now confirm, is good for our physical health. Reflective writing actually lowers pulse and blood pressure, increases T-cell production, and boosts the immune system. Writing can help us cope with chronic conditions like physical pain—and the loss of health, of dreams, and, yes, of children.

Most people believe in the benefits of exercising the body; stretching, toning, and sweating will keep us in decent physical shape. We forget that our minds also appreciate a good workout: the chance to make metaphor, track meaning, sift through experience, re-imagine. In fact, recent studies are proving that vivid writing stimulates different brain areas, making them light up, glow, connect.

We continue to marvel, over the years, at the gifts our words offer us. "I had no idea I would create that character," someone says, "or burst that myth about myself."

We have also witnessed firsthand how writing can help sculpt our experience. The novelist Lee Smith, who lost an adult son, said: "Simply to line up words one after another upon a page is to create some order where it did not exist, to give a recognizable shape to the sadness and chaos of our lives."

Almost from the start, the women knew they wanted to offer some of their stories to a larger audience, and I wanted to share the workshop methods that helped them flow. This then, is our offering: It's both a how-to book about leading a writing workshop—including many of the prompts, my own and those of others, that I've found effective—as well as a collective memoir of the group. The women have filled countless journals with anecdotes, responses to prompts, and notes to self. Excerpts appear throughout the book. When we're not together we correspond through email and Facebook. We've started a blog. Some of these exchanges appear here too.

If you are suffering, we hope you'll find familiar feelings in these pages, "aha" moments that will help you feel less alone. We encourage you to write in response to some of our prompts. Perhaps you will want to form your own writing group and use this book for guidance, as a step-by-step template. We also hope psychologists, social workers, chaplains, and grief counselors will turn to this book as a resource for their own personal and professional development as well as for their clients. Writers and writing teachers will find compelling prompts.

After all these years, when our group comes together now, we chatter and goof off, go swimming, take walks. Some of us like to play board games. We tease each other, chop vegetables, and cook. But as soon as we settle into our circle and open our laptops or notebooks, a hush comes over the room. So much has been revealed to us through the writing, so much shared. Our written words are the bond that truly hold us and uphold us; they are the glue. We breathe in and exhale, knowing we'll be surprised, moved, maybe even transfixed by what emerges on the page.

Eleanor Munro writes in *Readings for Remembrance*, "In a dark time, the best help is imagination, the mind lifted up like Noah's dove to wing its way to a restorative green tree."

Through writing we have found hope and creative sparks and healing and insight and laughter and tears and company and, indeed, restoration.

We hope you will too.

How This Book Works:

In **Snapshots,** I introduce you to the women in this group and some of their writings.

Salem College, Day One details our first meeting: each writing exercise and why I chose it.

Five Years takes the group forward through half a decade, focusing on our twice-yearly meetings, our deepening friendships, and, of course, our writing.

Weymouth Walk serves as an epilogue.

Prompts and Resources offers more materials.

I Want to Help shows meaningful ways other people stepped in, at our darkest hours.

SNAPSHOTS

When a woman tells the truth she is creating the possibility for more truth around her.
—Adrienne Rich

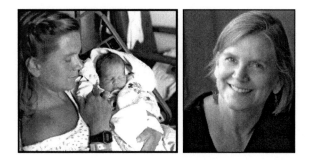

CAROL

Flannery O'Connor says you might save somebody else's life by writing and that, actually, the life you save might very well be your own.

Writing has saved mine. The scribbled chronicle I kept during my son's brief life provided the only tether to sanity during those free-fall hospital weeks. I could not thumb through the *People* magazines, watch the blaring televisions in the parents' lounge, or read the books friends sent. All I could do was sit by my son, stare at his beeping machines and tiny heaving chest, and write.

I wrote down everything: the overheard conversations between nurses and other parents; what the doctors told me, "Your son's heart defect appears in one in a million babies"; the tragedies unfolding all around me—like the one in the next cubicle where a baby girl with a cherubic face fought for her life, a rare disorder twisting her heart and tummy.

I've always found that once my words meet the page something shifts. The drama is no longer locked inside the trauma center that is my brain. Somebody else is in on all my secrets, shame and passion, even if it's only the pages of my journal.

"Better to write for yourself and have no public," said the critic Cyril Connolly, "than to write for the public and have no self."

Over a dozen years passed after my son's death before I pulled down the attic ladder and dug around up in the dusty heat for my boxed journals from that time. All I needed was a few ideas for parenting pieces, to fill out an essay collection.

I ended up with a memoir about my son.

At every reading I gave after the book came out, parents approached me, spilling their own stories and asking, sometimes pleading: "What can I do? I feel so empty, so lost."

At first I was paralyzed, deer-in-headlights, looking into their drawn faces—the business man in a crisp suit with lines under his eyes thick as the charcoal stripes football players paint under theirs; the Indian woman in an aqua silk sari with a red dot on her forehead and mascara-stained cheeks; the cute young couple who should have been getting voted "Most Adorable" in high school, not standing here in front of me, shoulders stooped, lips quivering.

Finally the words came to me. "Write," I would say, squeezing their hands. "Write and share your writing."

That's what I told the women gathered around the boardroom table at our first meeting, back in 2002.

"Write."

One of the first things we wrote that day—and everyone read aloud—was the stripped-down summary, fact by fact, of our children's lives. Here is mine:

"My first child, Malcolm McCranor Henderson, was born on September 22, 1982. He died on November 5, 1982, in his second open-heart surgery at Boston Children's Hospital. He was 42 days old."

Now you'll hear the women's facts, as they read them at our first meeting, along with excerpts from their writing and some of my early impressions of the group.

BEVERLY BURTON

"My sons Wesley Kyle Burton, we called him Wes, and Andrew Joel, we called him Andy, died six months ago in a car accident, on March, 29th 2002." Beverly spoke in a soft voice with a strong country Southern accent. *"Wes was 16, born on May 16, 1985 and Andy was 14, born on October 14, 1987."*

I had to admire Beverly for attending this workshop. Six months is a blink in grief time. Yet you would never have known, passing Beverly on the street or even seeing her seated here with the other women, the agony she was living. Straight-backed and pretty, with short blond highlighted hair and a tastefully made up face, Beverly looked unscathed. She was slim, her composure almost uncanny. The only tip-off might be that she picked her words with unusual care and spoke in a controlled deliberate voice, perhaps to hold back the flood that could rise and overwhelm her.

This accident was a particularly cruel crash in which three of the four boys involved, all good friends, died. Beverly was the mother of two of the boys. Another mother in the group, Kathy Shoaf, was Beverly's best friend and the mother of the other two boys. One of Kathy's sons died in the crash and the other, the only survivor, had been behind the wheel. Everybody in Winston-Salem seemed to know about the well-publicized tragedy and the boys' memorial services that brought out thousands of mourners.

In *The Year of Magical Thinking,* Joan Didion writes: "Life changes in the instant." One minute Didion's husband was sitting across the dining room table from her in their Manhattan apartment, sipping a second scotch. The next he slumped, mid-sentence, onto the floor, dead of a massive heart attack.

One minute Beverly was the mother of two teenaged sons; the next she was childless. The women in this group knew all too well that life changes, "in the instant."

In this excerpt, Beverly writes about a towering glass-doored box on solid oak legs that stands in her living room and holds mementos from her sons' lives:

"Living" on one shelf is a half empty can of Macadamia nuts, left by Santa in Wes' stocking on Christmas Eve 2001. The can was on his nightstand, by his bedside, and in just a little over three months, he had still not eaten them all. He was "savoring them," he told me.

Another item is the license plate the DMV allowed us to keep. But we didn't keep the Jeep, parked the night of the accident in his friends' driveway. In fact we never saw it again. That was Wes' most prized possession, a 1993 XC Jeep Cherokee, cherry red with champagne trim. He had paid for half of it and had only driven it for just over nine months. Several of his buddies had helped him install a lift, so he could go four-wheeling. The day before Wes died he took the Jeep to a muddy private field and had his last four-wheeling fun. He left the car that way, muddy. Some friends washed the mud away the day after his death. . . .

Still more things: the novel, A Tale of Two Cities, with a message, "this book sucks," scrawled by Wes under the title, and then whited out. . .

But Wes' things fill only half the case; the others were Andy's keepsakes. Golf balls, golf tees, his Ping golf hat, his golf course designs cleverly drawn in colored pencil. He spent lots of time alone in his room creating them. He told me a few weeks before his death that he had never been good at drawing, but for some reason he could draw golf courses. He said, "Maybe I can do this when I'm grown up, Mom."

When we were first meeting, email was a fairly new form of communication. A flurry of correspondence often circulated on email—and still does—around our children's birthdays and the holidays. Here's an email Beverly sent us all.

Another Thanksgiving—November 24, 2005

My husband was in a rather picky mood this morning, just trying, I think, to ease the burden of the day. I was watching the Rockettes perform in the Macy's Parade on TV, and he made some silly comment about them being sluts or something like that. For some reason I just burst into tears. I told him that his comment hurt my feelings. Crazy, huh?

I think he knew why I was crying yet we didn't acknowledge it to one another. My upset obviously had absolutely nothing to do with the Rockettes' being sluts, which I don't believe they are—and he doesn't either. I was just remembering the boys jumping out of bed on Thanksgiving morning when they were little to watch the parade on TV. When they were older it was football. And they didn't jump out of bed; they groaned their way out and certainly not before 10a.m.

Around 11a.m. Blaine and I made our way to K&W Cafeteria for a festive and soooooo delicious Thanksgiving lunch. Actually, it really wasn't bad and we were amazed at how many people were there. We had to wait over 30 minutes in line!

Then I remembered the only other time we had decided to make this day easier by not cooking. My mother was still living so it had to be at least seven years ago. The boys pitched a fit about going out for Thanksgiving, especially to a cafeteria. They called K&W the "k(c)anes and walkers cafeteria."

If they were here now, I would have prepared a feast.

So, today, our fourth Thanksgiving without Wes and Andy, we made it, one more time. Now we have to face the next holiday, the big one. How many times will I heave a sigh? How many tears will I cry? How many times will their names reverberate through my head, through my heart? I cannot answer these questions…and that is okay.

PEGGY CLOVER

Peggy was the only woman in the group I already knew; she had attended an earlier writing workshop of mine and had grilled me then about my experience writing a memoir. How much time elapsed after my son's death before I started writing the book? How long had the writing taken me? She wanted to write about her dead daughter and to compile her daughter's own writings.

A broad-faced woman with short dark brown hair, Peggy had big brown eyes that darted side to side as she spoke. Sometimes she'd purse her lips and put an index finger to her mouth as though the gesture would help her find the words she was looking for.

"Rebecca is the third of Mike's and my four children," Peggy read to the group, her voice breaking. *"Born on July 15, 1978, she was 18 when she died of complications from mononucleosis, on December 3, 1996. She was at home for Thanksgiving from her freshman year at Florida State University."*

The day after the first workshop Peggy emailed me:

For me, to have a pen and paper in front of me (to write or to draw) is my grounding force. I think more clearly with a pen, and I see more clearly when I draw. Most likely, others who would choose to attend this workshop might feel that way too. The writing is private, and if you choose to share, you can READ it...and even in reading...it is the second time you have seen it, so you are choosing to share, removing some of the threat of emotional meltdown. For me, there is a fear of being publicly emotional—not because I don't want to show it, but when I do, I can't express what I want to say, nor can I keep my thoughts clear.

Peggy doodled (intricately) on her journal pages. She was an artist who regularly enrolled in studio art courses at a college near her home in Raleigh, North Carolina. "I was taking a course when Rebecca died and all the students were so supportive," she had told me earlier. "I don't know what I would have done without that class."

For one art project two years after Rebecca died, Peggy created and smashed an expressive bust of herself, then mosaicked it back together, leaving pieces out to create scars and rough surfaces.

"I'll never be the same person again," Peggy said, "and it seemed fitting to reconstruct my sculpture with parts of me missing and my image permanently changed."

When Peggy was first married she taught kindergarten but quit to raise her four children, a job she adored—the more children around and the messier their projects, the happier she was.

I used this piece Peggy had written before the workshop as the basis for a prompt on our first day: Write about something that belonged to your child.

Rebecca's Shoes

Shoes get to go wherever we go. They can be purchased for a specific event, like a wedding, or to make a fashion statement, or simply for comfort. Basically they are emotionally neutral as far as I'm concerned. We use them, wear them out, and throw them away.

It is only when the wearer leaves this life that the old shoes take on new meaning—all worldly possessions becoming the souvenirs of the life and person who has been separated from us. These possessions are now laden with memories and emotions. Even the most common items suddenly become treasures.

Rebecca's shoes are so representative of her experience. She went through quite a collection of dance shoes between the third and twelfth grades—high-top jazz shoes, low-cut jazz shoes, black, tan what's the difference? I still don't know, but now when I see those shoes I am reminded of her determination. She convinced us to buy each pair. She mastered new dance steps, kept moving, and kept practicing, even when her tap dancing on the kitchen floor, stretching exercises using the kitchen countertops, and high kicks everywhere drove our family crazy.

She was notorious for losing and misplacing everything; shoes were no exception. And she always needed new shoes for new dances, different colors, different styles. And of course, growing feet meant frequent replacements.

Her everyday shoes, quite bold looking with clunky heels, gave her a couple of added inches. The sight of her shoes now reminds me of the way she walked, casually, yet confidently, her feet turned out like a dancer's.

I want to take a closer look at the rest of the trivia that is around me in everyday life. Take notice, and register it NOW in my mind. I want to be able to notice the little things about all my kids. I want to savor the moments that we are allowed to share in life's journey.

DOTTYE CURRIN

Right away Dottye made herself known to everybody. A short full-bodied woman in her fifties, with a dramatic Susan Sontag white streak in her thick dark hair, Dottye spoke her mind freely. I heard her telling a group before we got started that first morning that she had gone back to school in her late 30s, at Salem College, where we were meeting. She went on to earn a Master's degree, and to plan curricula for pediatric medical students. She was proud of her academic and professional achievements.

"Hell, I was a high school dropout." she said. "No way could I even *think* of going to college."

Dottye cried unabashedly and without apology during our "Just the Facts" introductions, clutching the Beanie Baby bear (our talking stick) with both hands and mindlessly stroking it. Despite her sobs or maybe because of them, I sensed she was solidly self-confident, at home within herself. She wasn't afraid of her emotions and made no apologies for them.

When it was her turn to introduce herself, Dottye's face twisted in a deep frown, her full lips in an almost pout. She read:

"My son, Alex Snyder, took his own life on January 31, 1994. He was 25 years old."

19

I could tell that Dottye was going to contribute a lot to the group. She spoke up right away and wanted to share her writing. An open and enthusiastic personality like Dottye's adds energy to a group, but sometimes a super outgoing person can, without meaning to, hog air space and silence others. Dottye held onto the bear and petted it, clearly wanting to say more.

"We will be doing a lot of writing today," I told her, moving things along. "So don't worry. You'll have plenty of opportunity to read what you write."

For "something that belonged to my child," Dottye wrote about Alex's many uniforms.

The first was Alex's beloved Dallas Cowboys uniform. Before each televised game, Alex (age 3) would lay out his uniform on the floor, just so, in front of the TV—the pants, the jersey, the shoulder pads, and finally the blue and gray helmet with a big star on the side. I can still see Alex standing with his hand over his heart as the National Anthem played. He stood right there, like a good little soldier, through the entire thing.

More uniforms came later: t-ball, little league baseball, pee wee football. A lot of heart and no talent and not even size to compensate for lack of ability. I remember him running his legs off to try to score, only to be tackled by his own team mates; he was running in the wrong direction. I remember that father in the stands at the little league game, screaming and cursing at my boy when he swung and missed on a count of 3 and 0. But Alex loved being a member of the team. If only they had known his heart.

Then scouts from Cubs to Webelos to full-fledged Boy Scout, the camping trips at Raven Knob, the stories he'd tell. The way he'd be so proud of his friends when they were awarded the Order of the Arrow. Alex never got that award. If only they had known his heart.

And then the US Navy, that sharp looking sailor who was so deeply patriotic. He wanted to be a hero, a medic; he was promised he could do what he wanted. But the recruiter didn't tell him about the tests. Those damn tests, which only your standard-issue could pass. Not someone special, someone extraordinary, someone different. If only they had known his heart.

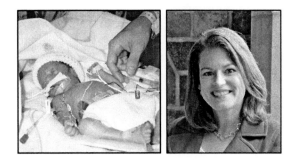

JULIE HESTER

Sometimes, a deep vertical crease formed in Julie Hester's forehead when she spoke. This line gave her pretty face a sad, worried look that belied her ironic sensibility. Her deep brown eyes locked right into yours, sometimes seeming to challenge. She was a no-nonsense type, frank. Funny.

"You think that I, a Presbyterian minister, knew where to look for help when my son died?" she told me. "Ha. I didn't have a clue."

"Our son, John Coffman, we called him 'Jack,' died when he was four days old on June 9th 1997 from a systemic infection. His twin brother, Hank, though also premature, survived."

Julie wrote about one of the few things that belonged to her son.

The Hat
It is small, white with a blue band around the turned-up brim. Knit or crocheted—I don't know which. Made by someone unknown, who took the time to create a cap for an unknown soul. Someone put it on Jack's head, I don't know who. A nurse, a doctor? I doubt it was my husband Dan. Jack was so sick, so in need of care, especially on that first day—it was hard to get near him. Babies lose a high percentage of their body heat through their heads, and one of the NICU goals is to help them learn to regulate their body temperature.

And so the hat.

Jack never needed to learn to hold in his body heat. He never learned to open his eyes, or cry, or nurse, or read, or ride a bike. He was already wise in other ways though—like some great Tibetan monk, a yogi, to whom others flock, just to be around, to gain wisdom.

In his hat, he held court. And others came: the nurses, the doctors. Dan kept a steady vigil except when he visited me, to share little bits of videotaped wisdom, in the other hospital, where I was, with Jack's twin, Hank. Our parents came, some sisters, a chaplain or two, and finally, me. The last day, I held the old soul in his new body, already so tired.

Every old soul needs a hat.

Maybe I need to get myself one.

In the next piece, Julie offers a picture of the almost absurd juxtapositions a bereaved mother faces as she tries to go about the business of living and caring for her other children. She is writing in response to the prompt given a few years after that first day: Think back to when you came to the first workshop.

It's a wonder I saw the notice about Carol's workshop at all. I didn't always have time to read the paper. Getting Hank to kindergarten and home, Lucy to preschool and home, then trying to work a little took up what time I would have otherwise spent at the kitchen table looking over the daily news. But that day I spotted the notice about the writing workshop for bereaved mothers. It had been five years since our son Jack died. And while I knew I really needed some help, all I told my husband was that I wanted to try some writing.

I called the number listed, left a message, and sort of forgot about it, figuring either the class would be full, or I had waited too long to register, or I wouldn't be able to get away to go anyway. The call back from Diane at Hospice came while I was in the car rider line at the elementary school. Lucy was asleep in her car seat in the back. My cell phone rang just as the line began to move forward, and I almost didn't answer it. It's not safe to drive while on the phone, right? I didn't want Mrs. Spencer to frown at me when she opened the door to let my son in.

Diane told me that Hospice wanted to talk to each mother before the workshop. I guess to make sure we weren't on the verge of some breakdown, or that our loss hadn't been the week before, although who would have been able to even consider sitting in a room with other bereaved mothers a week after? Right after Jack died, I just wanted to crawl into a hole and die, except that I still had a baby in the NICU who needed me to pump my breast milk.

But five years later I could talk on the phone, and I pulled around the circle, trying to answer her questions, wave competently to Mrs. Spencer, smile at Hank, and drive at the same time. Such was my life. Get through the necessary activity, appear capable and maternal and a safe driver, while talking objectively about my grief so as not to alarm those around me. But inside, there was a frozen place. I had no idea that I had just found a way to begin to thaw.

Beth Baldwin

Beth Baldwin's Moravian church was one of the sponsors for our first workshop. She told me later that she'd said to herself, well, why not go. "I never would have come," she said, "if my church hadn't been involved." I believed her. I sensed that Beth would feel more comfortable at a benefit, or a planning meeting for a good cause, than as a participant, someone seeking—or in need of—a service *for herself*. Beth was a provider.

She was tall and stoical, slim as a cigarette, with short wavy gray hair. Her clothes were neatly ironed and creased, her teeth white like the pearl studs in her ears. She smiled as she talked, her upper and bottom teeth touching but not clenched.

"Our middle child, Branner Baldwin, age twenty-six, died of melanoma on July 25, 2000."

Branner's VW Van

That pea yellow, rusty, broken down, 70s era, Grateful Dead VW van was Branner personified. I tried to get him to sell it and cursed the van's existence—junking up the circular drive in front of our house. Finally, I came to terms with it and accepted it as one of the family. I reluctantly admitted that it was "kind of" fun sitting on the cushioned benches in the back and bouncing around all over creation, the sink, fridge, and portable toilet keeping me company.

24

Occasionally, a sleeping bag would bonk me on the head, or a box of miscellaneous parts ordered from a special VW supply house in L.A. would careen by the window. Branner loved the pop top for camping and the jalousied windows that cranked out to let fresh air in, much needed to shoo away moldy, gross smells from hiking boots and old pizza boxes.

I miss that VW van; I never thought I could say those words. After Branner died, we sold it to the cutest young art student. I saw the van the other week at the School of the Arts. I ran up and rubbed my hands along its side. That's a demented thing to do, but then, I'm sometimes not quite right these days.

The guy we sold it to could have been Branner's soul mate: dreadlocks, slight smoky smell, sloppy jeans, and all. I wish Branner and Campbell could have met. Campbell says, "That van has good vibes." He took it out West last summer. Maybe Branner and Campbell have met—somewhere out in the Rockies—smelling the snow, shooting the breeze, thinking that life will go on forever, just like this.

All of us have written about the vortex of grief Didion discusses in *The Year of Magical Thinking*. Beth wrote:

The Vortex Effect

I prefer to call it spiraling. I always had spiral notebooks at school. In particularly boring classes like "Home Ec," I used to clandestinely wind the spiral out of the notebook, which took a bit of dexterity in itself, all the while pretending to be listening to "stitching your apron" instructions. Then came the hard part. I thought this should be an item on an I.Q. test. I would screw the wire back in the notebook, carefully threading the spiral through the vacant holes of the cover and pages, holes that had hopefully remained lined up in proper order, expecting to be reconnected and whole again. And there was one part of the wire that always stuck, the doubled over and bent end piece, a clumsy obstacle to an otherwise smooth process, yet so necessary to keeping the spiral in its proper position.

When I was sitting in a hospital room on a particularly cold, wet, and dreary day in Pittsburgh, I thought of those long-ago spirals and the pit that our family had spiraled down to – deep, dark, hopeless, and sad. Everything sane, familiar, and constant . . . life, itself, was spiraling out of control.

But the interesting other side is that spirals can also go up. This is the reverse hard part of putting things back together again. This procedure is longer and has lots of sticky ends that catch and obstruct. The process takes courage and perseverance and determination; it's an effort to join together the pieces once more.

KAY WINDSOR

"The youngest of my three children and my only daughter, Elizabeth Anna Windsor," Kay read, *"died in a car crash at five o'clock in the afternoon on October 11, 1996, less than half a mile from our house. She was born on December 31, 1980, and was fifteen years old."*

One of Kay's characteristic gestures was to rest her right hand, elbow bent, on her left clavicle as though she were saying the "Pledge of Allegiance" or trying to keep her heart from jumping out of her body. Sometimes she reversed the gesture and placed her left hand over her right clavicle. She wore glasses and had short brown hair; she looked like a friendly, almost timid, librarian. That first day she spoke in such a hushed tone we could hardly hear her. I knew she was a high school English teacher and wondered how she managed to discipline a rowdy classroom.

Something of Kay's daughter's:

In the still dark early morning a few hours after the car crash, I remember a telephone call from Carolina Life Care, the agency that coordinated organ donations. The caller gently asked if we would be willing to donate organs or tissue of Elizabeth's. We said yes, knowing that she had chosen to be an organ donor when she applied for a learner's permit.

"Sounds like the ultimate recycling," Lizzie had told me, as the driver's license official witnessed her choice. Although she was listed as DOA, dead on arrival (to the hospital) on the death certificate, some organ donation was still possible: heart valves and corneas. Four people were helped to see or live with Elizabeth's eyes and heart parts.

Three years after our first meeting, I read the women a prompt: an essay by Brian Doyle called "Joyas Volardoras" about hearts—human, hummingbird, and whale. Kay wrote:

Hearts and Hummer
The rainbow bearded thornbill
Has a heart the size of an infant's fingernail.
And it too may beat
Two billion beats before it stops.
But those beats happen in a flash, a flicker,
Like fast forwarding old movies
At a thousand frames a second
Instead of thirty-two.
The rainbow child of mine
had a heart the size of the Blue Ridge Mountains
And it beat
Some 70 million times
In fifteen years, nine months, and eleven days.
I long to rewind, pause, freeze-frame that child in time.
Instead I can only hold her in my heart.

By chance, a few months before our first meeting, Kay happened to find Betsy Anderson's self-published book on the Internet, *Fly On, My Sweet Angel*. It's a collection of letters others had written after Betsy's daughter Caroline Elizabeth died, and letters Betsy then wrote to her daughter. Betsy and Kay were drawn to each other—both had outgoing, blonde daughters who had died at almost the same age and who shared the name Elizabeth.

They agreed to meet for lunch at a restaurant on Interstate 95, halfway between Betsy's home outside Washington, DC, and Kay's in Winston-Salem, picking their meeting place by looking for restaurants on the Internet. The place they chose turned out to be a truck stop. Trying to ignore the quizzical looks from the truckers, they enjoyed greasy sandwiches and Diet Cokes together at a dark corner table. They became instant friends. When Kay saw the announcement about the writing group, she contacted Betsy.

BETSY ANDERSON

A slight woman with wispy fair hair, thin lips, and smooth porcelain skin, Betsy, like Kay, was also soft-spoken.

"My younger child, a daughter Caroline Elizabeth Anderson, got sick on Valentine's Day at her boarding school in Virginia. She died early the next morning, February 15, 1995 of meningococcemia after suffering the day before with what everyone thought was the flu. Caroline Elizabeth was 16 years old; she was born on September 23, 1978."

Betsy's response to "Joyas Voladoras":

My heart almost stopped as soon as I was born. My mother was told of me, the firstborn twin: Baby A isn't doing well. She's blue. The doctor was preparing her for my demise.

My heart started to crack when Daddy said he wasn't going to be living at our house anymore. He sat on my sister's bed in our shared room and told us that he had to leave, but he would have a house and a pony for us to ride.

My heart cracked further when the every-other-weekend-away-from- Mom turned into years, seven to be exact. My father's hurt heart was too soothed by alcohol, and his angry accusations became truth to his trusting daughters' hearts.

My heart started to mend when I became Mrs. A, with two children, a dog, and two cats.

My heart cracked open when my father's heart, long abused, but finally sober and happy, stopped one April 5th.

My heart broke one Valentine's Day in the midst of celebrating twenty-one years of marriage, a pledge to love, honor and obey interrupted by a daughter's goodbye. Her runner's heart ran its final race on a hospital bed.

I turned blue again and wondered, if, like Baby A, Mrs. A would ever survive a heart grown cold.

Here's an excerpt from the death narrative Betsy wrote, four years after our first meeting.

Her father and I were allowed to see her twice while the doctor and nurses in children's pediatrics tried desperately to save her life. The effect of this disease is devastating to the body. Meningococcemia causes skin discoloration and swelling. This occurs when blood vessels burst. Elizabeth was unrecognizable when Rick and I went in to see her after the intubation. We would not have known her at the end of her ordeal.

In life, Caroline Elizabeth had a glow that was hard to resist. I remember going to a debutante party in Washington and seeing her surrounded by attending naval cadets. She had a sparkling sense of humor and a touch of impishness . . . She seemed to turn everything into gold.

That said, I hope you can understand the tremendous impact her death had on her family, friends, and the community. As her mother, I felt a great responsibility to help relieve the grief of everyone around me. Only later, seven years later, when I came to be a part of the writing group in Winston-Salem, did I start on my own grief work.

It was at that first workshop that I cried for my daughter. It was there that I felt comfortable enough to let go of some of the pain of my Elizabeth's death. My tears surprised me that day. I had not cried much up until that point. I was too busy taking care of others. Even the book that I wrote about Elizabeth was written for her friends who were suffering so acutely.

I thought I had worked out my grief, that my emotions were under control. How naïve I was. There was, and I expect there always will be, much sifting and sorting of feelings and responses to her physical absence.

MONICA SLEAP

Monica was a Hospice nurse with classic Irish looks—thick black hair, freckles, and a pale complexion. Growing up, she and her six brothers and sisters were supposed to be quiet during dinner to give their mother, an oral surgeon's wife, a break. By making sly faces or pinching each other, the children competed to see who could make the others laugh or shriek, and get in trouble. Maybe it was around that crowded dinner table that Monica cultivated her deadpan expression. But she couldn't hide the sympathy in her green Spaniel eyes.

"My daughter Katherine Mary Sleap, we called her Katie, died in a car accident on her way to school on February 22, 2001. She was born on June 1, 1983."

Katie's was another accident familiar to those who lived in the Winston-Salem area. A senior in high school and an active student who played violin in the local youth symphony, Katie lost control of her car when she hit black ice on a country road. Many in the community thought the schools should have been closed that day or at least the opening delayed. They blamed the superintendent for poor judgment.

Monica wrote in her narrative about Katie's final day:

Katie was Co-President of the Girls Council and was anxious to get to school that day. As she headed down the hall to the stairs leading to the basement, she called back to me about our dinner meeting that evening. We had dinner every Thursday night before her recital practice with the Winston Salem Youth Symphony. That year I was serving as President of the Parent Committee.

"Would you mind if we went to Elizabeth's Pizza tonight for a change?" she called out.

"Sure," I said, "Meet you there at 5."

"Great," she said. "Thanks Mom. See you then. Love you."

That was the last time I heard her voice.

The school superintendent paid a visit to the Sleap family the night of the accident and expressed his deep regret and condolences. The family did not fault him. "Even if he hadn't come to our house and been so gracious," Monica told me, "we wouldn't have blamed him."

The Sleaps wanted the community to heal and to forgive. Monica's husband Rick wrote a letter to the editor of The *Winston-Salem Journal* trying to quell the rage over the superintendent's decision. Eventually the school-closing policy changed.

To this day Rick and Monica see pictures of their daughter flash by on the local news during discussions about winter weather conditions and related school closings.

Monica on "Joyas Volardoras":

Half My Heart

When I was in 7th grade English class, Sister Mary Grace instructed my classmates and me to pick a poem to memorize for an upcoming poetry contest. Parents and families were invited to attend the event, scheduled for the large auditorium. During the many practice sessions, I sat quietly at my desk with my poem, listening to the other eager students; they raised their hands to go first. When I finally stood in front of the class to recite my poem, Sister Mary Grace was pleased to see that I had chosen a poem that was not, like many of the others, "run of the mill."

The poem I chose, "Lasca" by Frank Desprez, was one my great Aunt Margaret used to recite during family holiday gatherings. I loved listening to her, the words carrying much emotion as the tale unfolded about a young man and woman riding their horses in Texas down by the Rio Grande. Unfortunately, the young lady lost her life in a stampede of steer.

Although I didn't win the contest, I have carried this poem with me in my mind ever since. I correlate its meaning to my feelings since Katie died: "I gouged out a grave a few feet deep, and there in earth's arms I laid her to sleep. And there she is lying and no one knows; and the summer shines, and the winter snows . . . And I wonder why I do not care for the things that are like the things that were. Does half my heart lie buried there?"

BARBARA GOLDSMITH

When we first arrived in the boardroom that October morning in 2002, I noticed that Barbara did not mingle with the others. She stood alone, reserved and watchful. She was tan and muscular, with short brown hair and brown eyes. She wore glasses and a rather stern expression. She seemed distant, perhaps shy. Sometimes I get nervous around people who are hard to read. Was she judging the group? This event? Me?

"My son William died of cancer on September 19, 1997," Barbara read. *"He was born on February 7, 1989 and was eight years old. At the end I cared for him at home. I'm a nurse."*

Seeking out a group like ours was out of character for Barbara:

I'm really not a "joiner." In fact, there is not much that I like less than being surrounded by a bunch of strangers, let alone strangers who have all lost children. And I don't like support groups. I think they tend to be about telling a worse story than the person who went before you. So in the five years after William's death, I didn't share my experience with many. Yet, I did see a grief therapist for about a year. And I would recommend that to anyone. Even if you think you're okay, let someone else tell you that you are.

I saw a small ad in the local paper with information about a meeting for bereaved mothers who would like to explore writing as a way to promote healing. I liked that thought. It sounded somehow "clinical" to me. Not a support group. Not a social outing. But a clinical exercise that I could participate in and perhaps find new avenues of outlet. But I really didn't want to talk to anyone or share private thoughts.

We don't always take into account how life evolves. We don't really plan to do some things, but they just happen. And so it has been with this group. After all our years of tears and laughter, there's nothing more sacred than what we reveal. I have found myself sharing such poignant moments that no one else would understand.

This is Barbara's response to a prompt to write from one of your children's points of view.

Love, or William's Story as I Imagine He Would Tell It

I think my mommy loves me.
Even though she wouldn't talk to the doctor who wanted to tell her about my cancer.
I never saw her act like that before.
But she stuck up for me after surgery.
She yelled at the nurses who didn't come when I called.
She finally said she would just do it herself.
She hung my bags of chemotherapy from the ceiling fan in the kitchen.
We made a bed for me in there.
She played games with me when it was time for a shot.
I acted like I was mad at her for hurting me with needles, but I think she knew I didn't really mean it.
I know my mommy loves me because she quit her job and stayed home with me all the time. She sometimes even slept with me. She bought me orange popsicles and Dr. Peppers. She bought me fireworks at Sparky's. Then she acted surprised when I'd sneak up on her and set them off.
I'm sure my daddy loves me, too.
Even though he had to go to work.
But when he got home, it was play time.
I think Daddy is really just a little boy in a big body because he really loves to play.

35

And he got every bit as excited to meet Michael Jordan as I did.

Daddy always treated me like nothing was wrong.

Even when the doctors said I should be careful because I could bleed easily, he still let me get up on the roof and hammer nails with him.

And he paid me ten cents per nail, too.

I really do believe my mommy and daddy love me.

There at the end, I tried to tell them.

I sat up and looked at them and tried to talk.

I just wanted to say that I knew they loved me but the words wouldn't come out.

I think they knew it anyway.

Oh, and Henry loves me too.

Henry's my dog.

I know he loves me because when my body was lying there, he climbed up on the bed and sniffed me up one side and down the other. Then he jumped off the bed and was sad.

I think he told me goodbye.

But the biggest way I know my mommy and daddy love me is what they did last.

They kept me at home for a few hours so my friends could come say goodbye.

Then my strong daddy picked me up.

He said he didn't want some strange men in a big black car coming to get me.

So he carried me through the kitchen.

But I was stiff and he couldn't get me out the kitchen door.

He had to bend my legs to make me fit.

He and mommy sat in the back of the big Buick station wagon and held me.

I was still wearing my Michael Jordan t-shirt and silk boxers.

My grandpa drove the car to the cremation place.

They wondered how they would explain if they got stopped by the cops.

They even laughed a little about that.

They asked the man to not take my boxers off, that I wouldn't like that.

It was hard for them to leave me.

But I know they love me because they went as far as they could with me.

I wish I could have taken them with me.

Because I love them too.

KELLY SECHRIST

Like almost everyone in the group, Kelly had reservations about coming to the first workshop. Besides having a toddler at home and living up in the mountains, she was also pregnant.

"My second child, a daughter Abigail Faith died from what was said at the time to be SIDS. Abby was born on October 23, 2001 and died on December 1, 2001."

Kelly had an animated pretty face, with deep dimples and a ready smile. Clearly the youngest, she could have been the daughter of many of the women, yet she seemed at ease interacting with everyone. She was fair-haired, with sparkly eyes, and very tall, the tallest in the group.

Kelly writes about remembering the first workshop.

I came into this grief group at the last minute. I waited as long as I could to call Hospice to sign up for the workshop. As an English teacher, I knew the merits of writing and especially the merits of writing about life, of telling my story, but I was not sure I could go to a workshop where I had to focus on me at this point. I had a two year old, a dead daughter, and a new baby on the way. Too many worries to count.

I drove around the roads in Old Salem three, four, five times before finally deciding I would stay. I carried a small tote with a notebook my mother-in-law had shoved into my hands as I left her house that morning and a crumpled, sweat dampened brochure for the workshop clutched in my hand. Damn it, I thought. The brochure doesn't give the specific details about where to park. Parking is driving me crazy. I certainly don't want to have to walk far. My pregnant feet are too swollen and tired, and I don't want to be here. I have a heavy heart and a heavy belly.

As I walked into the building that morning, I remembered another meeting I had attended several months before Abigail was born; our toddler mom's group had organized a discussion about the incidence of SIDS. I made a special effort that day to discuss the risks of this type of tragedy with the Director of Nursing, who presented. She said, "It happens, but it is so rare. We have not had a SIDS case in five or six years."

After the meeting, I pushed Cameron's stroller out of the hospital classroom with some reassurance, my pregnant belly bulging against the handles. Now, going to this writing workshop and carrying another big belly, I bitterly think to myself: that Director of Nursing did not know anything.

Kelly wasn't able to attend one of our later fall weekend workshops, the one at which we wrote about hearts, among other things. People sent her some of their writings and she sent this email to the group:

I hope everyone had a thankful Thanksgiving. We put up our tree last night, the one we bought and started putting up the day before Abby died. It is funny that putting up the Christmas tree on the Friday/Saturday after Thanksgiving had always been my favorite thing.

It's just so hard now.

Hanging all the special ornaments, particularly the ones we buy yearly for the children. That third little snowman, Santa, angel, that Abby will never show her children or hang on her tree or tell a story about or even see. Well, the tree is up and decorated, much to the joy of the boys and with sadness in Mom's heart.

Years later Kelly wrote about the death of a child in her community.

A three-year-old blond baby with little curls and a cute smile and big eyes died last week. She just had a little cold, a little cough, a little something. Then she was dead.

I don't know her family, but I do.

Everyone heard quickly—how many calls did I receive on Tuesday? First, the neighbor—hysterical. "What can I do for the mother? How can I lift her up?"

"You can't," I said.

Then it was my running partner. "The nurse practitioner, the one we didn't like; she was the one who saw her."

I picked up my pace.

Then my coffee confidante and cousin called, tentative. A whole new crop of conversation about Abby.

"Did you know that I washed your underwear the day Abby died?"

"No," I said.

"Well, I did and folded it too…"

My mother called next. "What do you know? Did the doctors mess up? What do you think?"

"I think that mom is devastated," I said, "and sobbing her eyes out."

I couldn't talk. Katie Gray was crying for apple juice. Cohen wanted to eat and Cam was reading to me. A normal family, right? Right?

Oh, did I mention the trip to the pediatrician's office? A doc stopped by. They have all been through so much with us.

"Can I ask you a question?"

"Sure," I said.

"When your daughter died (hesitation) when would you have liked the doctors to come together to meet with you?"

Am I supposed to be an "expert" on grief? I don't know what to think about all these conversations.

All I know is that it could happen to me.

Again.

Kathy Shoaf

Kathy had freckles, short red hair and a girlish wide face. Her saucer-shaped blue eyes were luminous and clear, her voice high and bell-like. I was not surprised to learn she was a soprano in her church choir.

"My middle child and younger son, Ryan died in a car accident on March 29, 2002," Kathy read. *"He was born on February 24, 1987 and was fifteen years old. He died in the accident with the Burton boys."*

For decades, First Street in Winston-Salem had been a favorite joy ride spot for adolescents. It featured all the thrills—a steep hill, a narrow road, and a bump that lifted speeding cars into the air. Driving fast along that stretch reminded kids of a rollercoaster.

Kathy's older son Wesley was driving the car with Beverly's boys in it and Kathy's middle child, Ryan. Wesley was the only passenger to survive the high-speed accident, the crash into a utility pole that tore the Honda in two.

Kathy imagined the accident's aftermath from Wesley's point of view:

I wake up in the hospital attached to an IV. Police officers and hospital personnel are asking me what happened. I don't know what happened. Why am I here? What's wrong? Where are the guys?

At last Mama comes in and I ask her, "Where are the guys?" I look on both sides of my bed. "Are they in another room?"

Mama says, "Son, they didn't survive the accident." "What!?" I ask and she repeats it; inside, I, too, experience sudden death. "Then I shouldn't be here either."

She tells me not to say that… that I must live. But I don't deserve to be alive. How can this be? My head hurts, I ache all over, I'm sleepy. I drift to sleep and wake up still in the hospital.

What am I doing here? Ohhhhhhh, Wes, Andy, Ryan…they're dead? This must be a nightmare. I have no memory of last night. They tell me that I was driving down First Street and lost control of my car. It hit a telephone pole and split into two pieces. How could this have happened? I am a good driver.

"Are you sure we were on First Street?" I ask over and over again. I just can't believe what they're telling me. I can't remember anything, but they keep saying the same things every time I wake up. I don't know what to say; I don't know what to do; I just want everyone to go away and let me die.

When we leave the hospital the next afternoon, I ask if we can drive by the scene of the accident on First Street. Mom and Dad agree. I just can't remember. What did we do last night? I can't remember anything after having dinner at Chili's. All these questions without answers haunt my confused mind as we drive.

Suddenly Dad stops the van and there it is, the scene of the accident. The telephone pole freshly marked by the impact of the car, skid marks on the street, splintered pieces of wood that only yesterday were part of a fence, now strewn across two yards. Oh, my God, it really happened. Wes and Andy, who were like brothers to me and Ryan, who was my brother, died here…because of me. I stare in horror as splintered pieces of my soul—that only yesterday were part of a happy, healthy life—splay across the universe. And the van bursts with a deafening silence. My head hurts, I ache all over, I'm sleepy. I want to drift to sleep . . . forever.

On coming to the initial workshop, Kathy wrote:

I was skeptical about this group when Beverly called on that late September day and invited me to participate. I am not a writer and it was only six months after the accident. But I was still so guilt-ridden I would have done ANYTHING that Beverly asked of me. We discussed riding together, but

41

decided to drive separately. If the day became too much I could leave at any time . . . That first day together was excruciating. When the group decided to continue meeting I declined.

Two years later, I was ready to rejoin. Everybody welcomed me back. Writing has been a healing experience. Getting the thoughts out of my head and putting them on the page, then sharing them with this group of women who truly understand, has been a great source of comfort.

SCHARME SHOWN

At the first workshop Scharme sat at the opposite end of the table, facing me. She was quite slim with sculpted brown hair and perfectly arched eyebrows. From the minute we sat down that first morning, I felt her penetrating blue eyes on me, staring and scrutinizing. I sensed desperation in Scharme, as though she were working really hard to stay in her seat, to not jump up and run out of the room.

"My son Steve was born on August 20, 1964 and died by suicide on August 23, 1999. He was 35."

Scharme writes about making the decision to attend our first meeting.

Who Could Understand?

Who could understand? Who could possibly understand? My phone rang, my life changed, forever. My son was gone. Steve was dead. Steve would never be coming home again. My world was colored "black."

How could this be? What do you mean Steve is gone? There would be no more unexpected drop-bys for a grilled cheese sandwich and a game of Boggle. There would be no more daily, "Hi, I love you. Have a good day," phone calls. No more Sunday tennis matches, impromptu cross country trips, or just a day to Cherokee for tubing and playing the slots. No more bear hugs and cocky (you

43

won't believe what I just did) smiles. Steve was gone and he wouldn't be coming home anymore. Who, on earth, could possibly know how I felt?

One day, anger, hatred, sheer outrage; the next guilt, remorse, denial, total disbelief, exhaustion from tears that seemed to be seeping from every pore. Friends' names eluded me. On the way to the park or the store, I would pull to the side of the road weeping. I forgot where I was going or didn't remember the way. Sleep. I was afraid to go to sleep. Sleep brought nightmares, horrific dreams of Steve's death. Sleep begat mornings—mornings meant facing reality once again. Steve was gone, gone forever except in my heart. I fought sleep.

My body felt as if it had been ravaged (and people told me that was exactly how I looked). Some days I was completely immobile, my body shut down. I didn't get up. At times the pain in my chest was so excruciating I was certain it was a heart attack—some days I wished it were. Others, I treaded water, struggling to keep my head above the surface. Some days it was as if someone had hands around my throat. I wondered if I would ever draw another breath. Who could understand these feelings? Who would want to?

How am I going to cope? I have a family to be concerned about, my other children, Leslie and Marc. They are in shock, their brother is gone; he was too young to die. They are thinking, "It could happen to us," and I am thinking, "It could happen to them." They are as worried about me as I am about them. How are we going to get through this?

I thought if I heard "time heals" one more time, I would scream. Don't they realize that time is not going to bring Steve back? No amount of time is ever going to do that.

I was in a very bad place. My therapist insisted on medication and/or hospitalization. There had to be a better way.

All these feelings and emotions were to be expected, I had read. They were normal. I felt anything but normal. I had to work through (not avoid) this. But how, where to start? So much bottled up inside. How do I let it emerge without being thought crazy. If anyone truly knew what I was thinking, they would surely lock me up. I felt trapped inside myself.

Then an answer to my prayers came through a friend who sensed I was ready for help. She suggested I call Hospice about a daylong workshop led by a writer and teacher who had lost a son. The session would focus on writing about grief. I was reluctant, I am not a writer, I wouldn't know where to begin. I was desperate. I made the call.

About our first meeting, in response to the prompt: I remember, Scharme wrote.

I remember thinking the day was passing too quickly; there were not enough hours. We were not done, not nearly done, in fact, we would never be done. Friendships bonded that day for a reason none of us would have chosen, either now or then. Healing progresses in the presence of unconditional love and understanding. I did not want this day to end. . .

We had started something beautiful and it was not finished. Carol made a proposal that we meet again in six months; without hesitation, we agreed. Another prayer answered, something to hold on to, even something to look forward to.

I remember what I took home with me that day. First, the knowledge that these were women who knew exactly where I was coming from. Second, a tangible tool to use each day—ways to write into and through my grief.

I don't use these techniques every day, but when I do, the day is better. Morning writings, before I rise, have served me well. These are a way of saying "good morning" to Steve. Some are happy, some are sad; but that spiritual contact with him enables me to begin my day on a more positive note. My writings are a living memorial for Steve each day and a purging of the soul for me.

I have been blessed with this group of women who lessen my pain through writing, sharing, and understanding. May you be so blessed.

Salem College, Day One

Be gentle with the one
who walks with grief.
If it is you,
be gentle with yourself.
                    —From a Celtic prayer

Morning

Saturday Night Live's Gilda Radner was right. It's always something.

I thought I was ready for anything. I had planned this workshop thoroughly; organized the day to unfold carefully, alternating between prompts that dug way down and those with a lighter touch. I had prepared clear guidelines and goals.

The "something" I hadn't considered, though, was the walk-in-freezer posing as a boardroom, the icebox in which we were supposed to write on this Indian summer Saturday morning. Everyone was dressed in cottony, light clothes. No one had thought to bring a sweater—or gloves and earmuffs.

"Welcome everybody," I said, my lips blue, my body literally shaking. "You are all courageous to be here, especially in these frigid conditions. By the way, I'm not nervous just cold."

Somebody called out: "We're cold *and* nervous." A few women laughed, giddily. Laughter is one of the greatest balms. The writer Anne Lamott calls it "carbonated holiness." None of us had a clue that laughter would become one of the deepest bonds among us.

I looked around the room at the group of women. Diane Spaugh, the hospice manager who helped me organize the day, had told me a little something about each woman. They had all registered, paid a nominal fee, and been interviewed by Diane to determine their readiness to participate in the workshop. Diane had also arranged for the building to be open for us and for us to have lunch in the cafeteria of this sylvan college campus.

But the cold? I had no idea what to do about it. No one else was in the building at 8:45 on this Saturday morning and Diane was not

49

available. I found a phone and a number for security but was told I couldn't change the thermostat myself; it was locked up, controlled in some central-headquarters Big Brother basement. We would just have to shiver until somebody, somewhere, cut off the arctic current.

Years later, several women admitted that they felt as cold on the inside that day as the air in the room.

I put my files and journal at the head of the long rectangular boardroom table, invited everyone to find a seat, and, shivering, slid into a chair at the head of the table. The women had been standing around in clusters, some talking, others just lingering alone—against the walls. As they settled into seats I smiled and gazed at the group, taking a head count. Everyone was here, which doesn't always happen: With the best intentions people sign up for a grief writing workshop, but when the actual day rolls around they push the snooze button, pull the covers up, and snuggle deeper into their warm sheets. Sometimes it's just too darn hard to show up.

On the first meeting of a writing group of this kind I prefer to have everyone sitting around a large table—this piece of furniture acts as both a barrier and a shared space. Some workshop leaders like chairs in a circle and lap writing, but I want the solidity and boundary of a shared table. The distance between writers is measurable, set. It's a solid surface on which to write without having to balance a journal on one's thighs.

"Help yourselves to these," I said, pointing to the three boxes of Kleenex on the long table. Some women already had. "I never offer a writing workshop of any kind without them."

A few of the women smiled weakly. Some dabbed at their eyes. Others wept. "Writing unleashes emotions, even when we least expect them," I said. "And today we probably expect them."

GUIDELINES

I pointed to the list of guidelines I had posted in large letters at the front of the room. Up and down the table, taut faces, some blotchy and tear-streaked, looked up at me as I read the list.

- Confidentiality rules. What happens in the room stays here.
- Follow your thoughts on the page.
- Read only what's written on your paper.
- Respond to the writing, not the emotion behind the writing.
- Our focus is on writing and sharing our written words.
- This is not a therapy group. It's a writing group.
- This writing is for you. You can tell the truth. Let it rip.
- Listen devoutly—to yourself and to others.
- If an exercise feels too uncomfortable, write about something else.
- Contribute only if you want to.
- When talking, be of lean expression. Focus on the reader's experience as expressed through her words, not on what her words remind you of in your own life. Save those thoughts for your journal.
- We all have the inner resources to take care of ourselves.
- You don't need to take care of anyone else today.
- Ask before hugging.
- Refrain from telling others: "It's OK." Often it's not OK.
- Writing about deep matters improves your immune system and lowers pulse and blood pressure.
- Remember: We have all "been there."
- Counseling and other resources are available through (name of counseling center and phone number).

"I will stick to these," I said "and will remind you to."

Psychologist Carl Jung said that for healing to occur, fear must abate. I needed to create a haven, a refuge, for these mothers. Writing can be like a bowl of warm soup on a drafty damp day. But everyone had to feel safe. They wouldn't be able to ease into their thoughts, and let images waft up from inside, if they were worried because someone constantly talked out of turn and wasn't stopped, or one member of the group tried to take care of everybody else, or something else distracting was happening in the room.

At each woman's place I had put a dappled composition book and a pen. Along with the Kleenex were boxes of colored pencils and highlight markers.

"Get settled in your chairs, as much as you can in this igloo." I said. "The first thing we're going to do is to create a healing place, a secure domain, in our journals."

HEALING PLACE

I told the women that I loved being read to and hoped they did too. "I'm going to start by reading a short excerpt from my memoir, *Losing Malcolm: A Mother's Journey Through Grief*," I said, "about creating a healing place."

Holding up the book, I showed them how much I was going to read—letting them know the excerpt was only a few short paragraphs. This gesture wards off troubling thoughts among participants like, "Oh no. She's going to read on and on." or "Is this workshop all about her and her book or is it about us?"

You don't want people having these thoughts, even flickers of them.

I've found that reading aloud can trigger people—a woman in an essay workshop once wrote about hating to be read to. No wonder. Her cruel older sister, who insisted on putting her to bed most nights, read her terrifying ghost stories.

"Write about being read to," is a good prompt but not for these women at this time.

I read to them about my healing place, an imagined inner landscape where I could go at any time, a sanctuary that brought relief and a sense of calm. I told the women that the imagery still works for me; it helps turn down the buzzing in my head, lowers the stress dial.

After my son died, I worked briefly with a grief therapist who offered a guided imagery exercise I later jotted down in my journal. Her purpose was to help me create a place where I could meet with my dead son. I did not "go there" with these women at our first meeting—I did not invite them to ask their children to join them.

My experience has taught me this: a person dies; the relationship does not. But to ask them to also invite their children into the scene in the first writing activity would have been going way too far, too fast. I only wanted them to find a retreat, a secret garden within themselves, for themselves.

Here's what I read:

"I felt blank. And then, suddenly, a setting appeared in my mind's eye. It was the field behind a house on Cape Cod, where Bill and I had often spent time as house sitters. Later I found a postcard of the view and tacked it to the wall in the back room where I wrote. In it, a grassy, tree-filled backyard is bounded by a low stone wall. Beyond, the wide meadow slopes down to a salt pond. Closer to the house and centered in the field, a lone cedar rises, straight and regal, out of the tall blond grass.

In my imagination, I place myself at the top of the yard, looking out and away, toward the pond. I try to smell the meadow—the dry sage sweetness mixed with the slightly briny odor from the salt pond. I feel the gentle breeze, the soft air rustling up from the water, making the meadow grasses bend and wave. I imagine a warm day, a deep blue sky."

Closing the book I paused—no need to rush today.

Silence is another of those magical elements. Like tears and laughter, silence can be sacred. Too often it is scarce—and unnerving. The poet Adrienne Rich writes that silence "can be fertilizing, it can bathe the imagination, it can, as in great open spaces, I think of those plains stretching far below the Hopi mesas in Arizona - be the nimbus of a way of life, a condition of vision."

"Just breathe into the silence," I said, "and enjoy our space." At last, some larger power had reset the thermostat, made the temperature hospitable.

"Feel your bottom in your chair, your feet planted on the floor, and your head opening up to the sky," I said. "Let an image of a special place, your own healing place, come to you. When you see it, and feel it, open your book and begin to write. Allow as many of your senses as you can to be involved—what are you seeing, hearing, smelling, touching? Does the air have a taste?"

There's no better terra firma than the sensory world. We interpret the world first though our senses, so they make a good starting point for writing. With a different type of group (and a more casual gathering), I might give as the first prompt something like this: Write about what's in front of you, literally. The composition book, your pen, a long wooden table. Take off from there.

I suggested they try writing in the present tense, "I sit. . .", that it can make the experience more immediate, more vivid. And I told them we'd spend about ten minutes on the exercise. It's always good to give a time frame for a writing exercise, especially early on in the day. (In the lifeguard training I took years ago, we all appreciated hearing we would only have to tread water, fully clothed and in boots, for five minutes.)

Every pen scribbled across the journal pages. If I had seen someone not writing I would have said something like, "If no images are coming to you, simply sit—or write about what *is* in your mind."

Always encourage everyone to feel adequate and equipped, wherever they are.

And it's a good idea to give a reminder as the time is ending. "Take about two more minutes." If everyone is still writing when the time is up, I might extend for another minute or so. In some workshops I set a timer but I chose not to here. I didn't want these women to feel pressured or startled by a closing noise. They were fragile as feathers.

Creating a healing space helps ground people, gives them a private haven of their own words that they can always return to. It reminds them that they have a self and a center, even if they sometimes lose track of these inner resources. It is also a creative, tactile exercise right up front that helps people understand that they do hold concrete and helpful landscapes within themselves, and the words to express them.

When most of the pens had stopped, I said, "You can read this to yourself any time today—and later, if you feel the need or the desire. You'll also have the chance to share it, and other writing too, with the group."

JUST THE FACTS

I asked the women to turn to a fresh sheet of paper. "Now write just the facts about your child who died: What is your child's name? When did your child die? How did your child die? That's all. By way of introduction, we'll read what we have written."

The women bent over their books and wrote. The Kleenex boxes passed up and down the table.

In a writing workshop of any kind, I feel it's important for everyone to write and read aloud near the beginning of the session. I always have people write their introductory remarks. Rambling spoken introductions use up gobs of minutes, get rambly, and give blowhards too much airtime. The talking also shifts the focus away from writing. In my workshops, it's all about the writing, beginning with these written and read intros. Every voice gets heard right up front. Contributing later will seem less intimidating, when they've done it once already.

After most of the pens stopped, I told the women that I would read first. That way I could model the behavior I wanted for this exercise.

I read my facts, then paused. Again, no need to rush. Let the words sink in. I passed the little red Beanie Baby bear I was holding to Peggy Clover, who was sitting on my right. I didn't want to be in a hurry, but it's important to keep the flow moving, especially in the introductions. Instead of waiting and having the women agonize over who would volunteer to read next, I went around the table writer by writer.

"When you have the bear in your hand," I told them, "you have the floor." This "talking stick" device has been much lampooned, but it controls discussion in a flexible, amiable way (What's more friendly than a teddy bear?). The bear was also something to hold on to, another grounding force.

"Take as much time as you need to read your words," I said. "And read only the words you wrote—what's on the page in front of you. Remember, we are here to focus on writing today."

You can't remind people too often just to read, not interpret, what they've written. We all want to supplement our words with chatter—and disclaimers. "This is sucky, but..." "What I really want to say but didn't write is..." If someone strays into explanation, gently stop her. Clear boundaries and kind enforcement of the rules are non-negotiable. Without them, trust won't grow in the room.

The little red bear made its way around the table. Everyone had the chance to be heard and to share just the briefest information about their children's lives—birth dates, cause of death, and death dates.

Had I simply given everyone an invitation to tell the group about themselves, their dead children, and why they were at the workshop, we could easily have spent most of the morning listening to each other's stories–and exploding into grief. I wanted to start simply, just the facts, contained.

That task alone took plenty of courage. It also kept the borders clear and clean.

I've been in writing groups led by others where people talk— telling each other the tale that's been whirring in the head ever since the accident or the illness or the suicide. Or they'll talk in detail about the story they plan to write. This could, I suppose, have a positive therapeutic effect, but not much gets written. We had gathered to *write,* I told the women, to converse with ourselves *on the page,* and to read our writing aloud if we chose. We were not here to chat.

In a more general reflective writing workshop, I might invite people to respond to the prompt: "Why Write?" Or "Write about your name." Or read the George Ella Lyon poem, "Where I'm From," and invite group members to write their own version of where they're from. Or have them pull three items from their wallet and write about them.

But in this group, the elephant was already in the room and did not have to be coaxed out: It was death, the death of their children. This was true for every one of them, without exception, so I could proceed, confident that everyone was not only curious to know something about the others, but already knew what that "something" was, and that's where we began.

For each of the women, even the briefest possible rendering of these huge facts brought powerful emotions to the surface. I embellished the prompt with a couple of extra facts—where my son died, that he died in surgery, and exactly how old he was. Many in the group will need to do this, and it's fine: a few extra words can be permitted as long as they're written.

Some were too overwhelmed to read their own brief information about their children's lives and deaths and, at my suggestion, passed their notebook to one of their neighbors to read for them.

I thanked each woman after she read, and gave special thanks to those who read for someone else. When we had gone all the way around the circle, I thanked everyone again. This is important; your workshop people will need this, especially following this critical first sharing. Not only does everyone deserve thanks for participating and following directions, coming from the workshop leader the gesture will remind the writers that someone is in charge.

What happens early on sets the tone. I think of Malcolm Gladwell's book, *Blink*. How quickly we make crucial, binding decisions and judgments. In a blink. Writing workshop time is rare. You want people to be fully present and confident in the workshop process.

What You've Just Heard

"Thank you all," I said, again. "You are brave to be here and brave to read or to try to."

Even though it might have seemed obvious, it was important to *name* what was going on. The women *were* courageous. In this context, I once heard a therapist refer to the fairy tale, "Rumpelstiltskin." Finding out the angry little man's actual name freed the queen from the promise she had made to him years before—that he could take her first child. Naming helps us be conscious and trust in our perceptions of what's happening.

"Now write about what you've just heard," I said. "What sticks with you? What do you remember from each other's readings? What has moved you?"

"Everything," somebody said. Others nodded their heads. So many children dead, one report right after the other; the facts were devastating but it was important for us all to know. We would be able to concentrate better on the writing if we weren't speculating, all day, about each other's facts.

Writing on the heels of listening gives everyone a chance to process the ideas, feelings, and thoughts that have been triggered by each other's words. The more startling or difficult the material, the deeper and more insightful the response writings are likely to be. This technique of turning to one's journal to process is an idea I was hoping to engender.

For these women, I knew that writing about not just their own, but also the other women's experiences would build on the "you are not alone" theme I wanted to cultivate. In addition, it would dissipate the emotional charge the readings had evoked and give the women a chance to compose their thoughts before we moved on.

I told them that by writing we air what's on our minds; we share it with the page. As soon as words are down, they don't have the same power over us. Our thoughts exist elsewhere and can be referred to, modified, explored.

Finally, once again, the act of writing reinforced the theme that this was a *writing* workshop. Always, always, we come back to the writing—to what's on the page, because that's the surest way I know to untangle our thoughts, about everything.

"Look, then, into thine heart and write," said the poet Henry Wadsworth Longfellow.

I told them we would write for about five minutes. The time might stretch to ten or maybe even fifteen minutes, and you can let it, if most of the writers are still scribbling at the five-minute mark.

Why then say "five?" if you might very well go over the given time? Because should you say, "fifteen minutes," at the outset, it will sound intimidatingly long, especially at the very beginning of the day. Keep segments short, manageable. If you give extra time, let them know you're aware you've done it.

What's in Store?

At my gym I've noticed that the most popular bicycle "spin" class is the one where the teacher tells us up front what we'll be doing for the entire hour. That way we know what to expect; we can parcel out our energy, knowing which climbs and sprints are coming next and when we'll have time to recover, hydrate, and regroup on flat terrain.

I believe in doing this with writing workshops too. It's important to let the group know, early on, how the morning, or day, or week will unfold. What to expect.

"Here's how our group will work." I told them. "As we go, I will be giving you a prompt of some kind. You'll write, then we'll move on to the next prompt. We will take regular stretch and snack breaks. At times I'll invite you to share your writing, but only if you feel inclined."

I nixed the idea of inviting comments on the writing immediately after the readings—as in: Let's discuss what's strong, what's memorable in the work, that sort of thing. We would simply listen and pause between readings. Everything was going to be evocative and memorable, and I was concerned that discussion could easily stray from the written words—into overwhelm and meltdowns.

Their notebooks, I told them, were private. No one would require them to read anything they wrote. No one would look over their shoulders to check their grammar or spelling. We weren't in school. As Anais Nin said, "The diary is a place where you don't have to worry about being perfect."

Forget about topic sentences, commas, and orderly thoughts.

"There is no right or wrong way to keep a journal," I said. "Let your pen flow here on these pages. Try to let yourself be spontaneous, honest, and deep. Try not to censor yourselves. These pages are for you. The best audience for your journal, as Tristine Rainer says in *The New Diary*, "is you and your future self.""

SENTENCE STEMS

The sentence stem is an excellent journaling prompt to use early in a session. Participants get a structure—the beginning of a sentence—something other than the glaring blank page. They don't have to worry about "getting going." You set them up at the starting line, fire the gun, and open the gate. All they have to do is run. And they will. Before they know it, they've been eased into expressing themselves more easily: in just a few fragments, a torrent, or a single word. The exercise can be tailored to the focus of any group.

Start a sentence and ask each of your group members to finish it: "A teacher might have described me as___" "Growing up, my family believed___" "I was expected to___" "The first time I experienced death was___."

Particularly relevant to this group were these, which came at the end of the exercise: "Nobody wants to hear about___" "I can't possibly tell anyone ___" "The hardest thing to accept is___"

Stems encourage writers to think in tiny pieces. All they have to do is complete the opening thought. "You can make lists in response to the stem," I said. "You can jot down ideas and leave blank space around them on the page, swing back and write more later."

LISTS

I love lists, use them all the time—lists of the emotions I'm feeling, lists of what I'm seeing in front of me, thoughts, the important moments from a day. Lists don't take a lot of time or require thorough fleshing out. It's a form of shorthand that clears the head, gets things down for further exploration later, and the act of making a list relieves pressure.

I like giving myself a number. "This will be a list of five." A few years ago, as I sat in my parents' bedroom, I wrote:

Nine reasons why I'm having such a hard time visiting them this time in their retirement home.

By item number seven, I was exhausted, but I forced myself to keep going. I'm glad I did: on number nine, I hit pay dirt—what was *really* hard.

I keep a notebook devoted to lists, making them in the car, at my desk, in waiting rooms. Even in the middle of the night, you can make lists of dream images or concerns—without having to wake up entirely.

At this workshop, since our focus was on exploring grief and healing, we started with a list of fears. "Write at least three," I said. Had this been a different type of group, I might have asked then to make a list of four childhood memories. Or a list of places they had lived, schools they had attended. Each holds a trove of stories. Here's a good idea for centering: list three things that matter, right now.

One of our lists that day: "The five things I miss most about my child." It was perhaps the toughest list any of us had ever made. It's important to have a variety of possibilities ready and to tailor the list topics to what feels right at the moment.

I ended with: "Make a list of three things you're grateful for at this moment. You may be grateful the room isn't freezing anymore, that the test came back negative, that your pen has ink, that the sun is slanting through that window over there. Small things or vast, anything about which you feel gratitude."

It's good practice to end with something positive—but in a group like ours, even an upbeat prompt must be considered carefully. For example, I would avoid: "Make a list of what you're looking forward to." I took care not to ask these women because I knew many were not looking forward to anything.

How Many Children Do You Have?

After a short break, I gave a prompt that I know can be devastating. "Write about this," I said. "What do you say/feel/think when someone asks, 'How many children do you have?'"

I suggested they might want to make a list of comments people had made; situations in which they've felt vulnerable and why; times they'd been able to talk about all the children in their family.

A few of the women sat still, looking at their books not writing. Others wrote immediately.

I always tell group members to feel free to sit and reflect before or after writing, and to enjoy the so-called idleness. "If your neighbor is writing madly and you've finished, fine. Just sit and try to breathe. And try to remember that comparisons are odious."

I'll ask, "How often do we give ourselves the chance, in this cacophonous world, for quiet and contemplation? To focus on what's happening inside us? To let our shoulders down and do nothing? Take the time. It's yours."

BEFORE AND AFTER

I wrote the word "Before" on the left, drew a line down the middle of the white board, and wrote "After" on the right side.

"Let's hear words that describe life before your child died," I said.

"Safe." "Happy." "Together." "Innocent." "Naïve." "Whole." "Excited."

I wrote the words on the board as the women called them out. Now think of words for the right side, the "After" side: "Broken." "Faithless." "Alienated." "Raw." "Insane." "Terrified." "Lost." "Alone." "Abandoned."

A group exercise like this, where everyone contributes words, builds a sense of community. People nod at each other. "Oh yeah. I hadn't thought of that."

Something else happens too. Considering a time "Before" allows a writer to remember another time of life. "Before this happened I was . . ."

Writing from "Before" is like climbing a stepladder and looking down at yourself from another perch. "Before, I actually enjoyed getting up in the morning." The possibility is there, even if dimly— that at some time in the *future*, you just might, maybe, have a different view. The utterly bereft mess who is writing at this table might be able to scoot over and make room for . . .

Shifts in perspective are some of reflective writing's shiniest nuggets.

"Pick a word from the "Before" list and write about it " I said. "Take about five minutes."

I reminded them to use concrete language. "Driving down Hodge

Road I admired the white blossoms on the star magnolias." Or "I walked upstairs without dreading the Bruce Springsteen posters staring from your bedroom wall." Or "The hummus tasted sharp, made my eyes water."

We did the same with "After."

ACROSTICS

When we wrote about "Before" and "After," I gave the option of using an acrostic. To make an acrostic, you write a word vertically down the page and use each letter as the beginning of a new line.

Why acrostics? They offer a simple frame and a pre-set structure, the letters. And then complete freedom for what comes next. Forms like the acrostic, I've found, can quickly tap deep and let the sap flow.

And there's the harbor of the next letter, to bring the writing back.

I always demonstrate by taking a word and creating a quick acrostic. I chose from our "Before" list, "Safe." Write the letters first, then fill out the lines:

Summers felt soft back then, velvety,

At Saranac Lake. We thought we were

Far removed from

Evil

Everyone can see that I'm making up the phrases as I go and this gives them more confidence to try the process. And it is just that—a process. No one expects a finished poem. Sometimes people write an entire paragraph for each letter. That's fine too.

BREAKS AND READING ALOUD

A must: Don't lose sight of ordinary human physical needs. Allow time for breaks—to stretch and graze (do provide snacks), use the restrooms, and look out windows. Let them know ahead of time: "After this exercise we'll take a break."

I've attended workshops where some brave and small-bladdered soul will finally raise a hand and say, "May we please have a bathroom break soon?"

Also, give writers the opportunity to read aloud. In this workshop, where the focus was to encourage honest probing on the page, hearing others read was an unexpected bonus—and a chance for bonding. As in: "I am not the only utterly insane woman on the planet."

I waited until we'd done several exercises, and they'd had a chance to settle into their thoughts, before inviting readings.

Note: We write differently when we're writing to share.

If one gutsy person reads, others usually pipe up. In this group, many were eager. We didn't have time to hear from everyone that morning. This will happen. Make sure those who haven't read, but want to, get to "go" before others read a second time.

"Go," is a word I hear often. "I'll go," somebody will offer, as she flips back through her notebook to the beginning of her piece. "Great," I'll say. "Thank you." It's such a privilege to hear the inner meanderings of another's mind.

Note: At all of my workshops, I try to pay attention to every single thing that's going on in the room. My motto, after Henry James, is to "be someone on whom nothing is lost."

It's an impossible ideal, of course, but a necessary goal.

REFLECTIONS AND LUNCH BREAK

After the women had read, I asked them to write a reflection about what they had just heard from each other. After that I promised them we would break for lunch.

I had cautioned the group not to discuss the writing over lunch unless someone asked specifically for feedback or wanted to discuss something she, the speaker, had written. In other words, don't pry but if someone wants to talk about her own work, that's okay. One of my mentors, Pat Schneider, insists on this and it's an excellent policy. Maintain boundaries. And remember: What happens in the writing space is sacred and stays among the members.

So, over soup, sandwiches, and brownies we made small talk. Many of the women were from the Winston-Salem area; some of them talked about people they knew in common; one woman realized she had rented an apartment from another years before; there was some discussion about dorm food and college life.

As we bussed our trays, I suggested people walk around the campus for the next twenty minutes—the day and the grounds were dazzling—then we'd meet back in the library boardroom.

AFTERNOON

I took another head count after lunch. They had all returned. If someone had not come back, I would have commented and let the women know that I would be in touch with the person after the workshop. Again, name what's going on.

We started the afternoon off with some deep breaths followed by ten minutes of quiet time: a chance for the women to look through their composition books and see what they had created during the morning session.

They thumbed through their pages, wrote, circled words, highlighted phrases, blew their noses and dabbed their eyes.

My only rule: no talking.

DIALOGUE WITH AN ASPECT OF SELF

Dialogues allow us to give voice to parts of ourselves we don't usually enjoy engaging with—stuff we try to censor, ignore, or sweep into the garage. I often dialogue with procrastination. Another good topic for me is money; another, my clamped jaw.

"I love this exercise," I said, "giving these inner pieces of us a chance to speak up. They can be bossy and sassy and uncanny. They almost always surprise us and teach us important things about ourselves."

It's a good idea to warm writers up by starting with sentence stems that help them hear their inner thoughts: "When I'm happy a voice in my head says . . ." "When I'm feeling self-critical, I tell myself . . . "When I'm feeling wise I notice . . ."

Move on to: "Whose voices do I hear in my head? My mother's? My older sister's? My child's? What do they say to me? Write all of this down."

Ask: "Is there a part of my body that's bothering me or seems to want to tell me something? Which part? Why?"

I then had the women isolate three emotions or feelings or concerns that they were experiencing or that the day had stirred up. I suggested they might want to have a dialogue with one of these.

I then read an example from another workshop, of a woman's dialogue with self-consciousness. I also read a dialogue from *The New Diary*, with the creative self. It's important with this exercise to give examples of actual dialogues.

"Use a playwriting format," I said, and demonstrated on the board. Name, followed by a colon, and a remark. Then the dialogue partner's name followed by a colon and the response.

I suggested it was a good idea to start with a question, to use the dialogue as an inquiry into an aspect of self. I wrote a sample dialogue on the board, making it up as I went along:

ME: Why are you always around keeping me from doing things?
PROCRASTINATION: Because you're so easy to hang out with. You do whatever I tell you to, without a fight.
ME: But I'm tired of you and you keep me from crossing things off my list.
PROCRASTINATION: You and your lists!
ME: Hey. What's wrong with lists?
PROCRASTINATION: You make them and feel all proud of yourself and then what happens? They sit around collecting coffee stains. . . .

And so on.

"Spend a few minutes thinking about what aspect of yourself you want to dialogue with," I said. "And then go ahead and start. Just see where this exercise takes you. You may be somewhat alarmed at the bold or irreverent voices that talk to you. Try not to hush them."

After about fifteen minutes I told the women to begin coming to an end. I said. "Ask your subject, whatever it is, if it has anything else it wants to tell you. Make sure to give your subject the last word."

Dialogue topics that afternoon included: Random Thoughts, Staying Busy, the Woman Who is Always Right (AR), Grief, and Fear.

Beth Baldwin wrote a dialogue with love.

ME: How do I know you anymore?
LOVE: How did you ever know me?
ME: Let me count the ways - a first kiss, a close family, precious children, life was good.
LOVE: So what has changed? I'm still around everywhere, like cupids at Valentine's.
ME: I've lost a big love in my life, and I'm not sure I know how to love anymore. I'm stoic and cold and unfeeling.

LOVE: So, take a sauna. Get in the hot tub. That will loosen you up.

ME: I'm cold on the inside, not on the outside in this ninety-degree weather.

LOVE: You are right; I can't come on the inside, unless I'm invited. You've got to want me to come in.

ME: I want you to be in my heart, but maybe I'm not ready to invite you in. I need a precipitous event, a turning point.

LOVE: Try this on for size - try holding your new grandson in your arms without inviting me in.

ME: Touche! my heart is glowing. Is there anything else I need to know from you?

LOVE: I never left you.

It Belonged to My Child

I asked the women to think of something that belonged to their child and write about it—a description of what the item looked like could be a place to start, or what it meant to the child.

Writings in response to this prompt appear earlier in some of the women's introductions.

Here's a piece by Betsy Anderson about her daughter's fleece:

The week after Elizabeth died, my mother and sister came over to the house to help me sort out Elizabeth's clothes. I was still in a daze of early grief and anxious to create sense out of chaos. I wanted to do the right thing for my daughter's sake, to carry on, as she would have wanted me to. That included getting my life back in order. I became a person I was not before: organized. It was as if my life depended on an orderly existence. It's no surprise that I later became a children's librarian.

At any rate, we made piles of clothes for her cousins. Lisa would get the big shirt, Anne would get the skirts, and on we went. There was one item, among a few others, that I had to keep, Elizabeth's L.L. Bean fleece jacket.

Five months before she died, my husband and I gave Elizabeth this fleece jacket for her sixteenth birthday. She loved that jacket and wore it everywhere. It became part of her uniform: fleece jacket, jeans and her high top boots.

Those were the clothes she was wearing when she went to the hospital the night she became so sick. In the midst of her excruciating pain, she asked the nurses not to cut off her fleece jacket. It was returned whole to us hours later, wrapped in plastic, as we said goodbye to her body.

I've wrapped my body in her fleece on many occasions since then. Navy blue, with an aqua snap opening, it goes with me everywhere. It has been to damp,

cold England to visit my English relatives, to Stonehenge in the pouring rain, to a French chateau with cool crisp evenings, to a breezy sailboat ride in the English Channel, to Jamaica in a tropical storm.

My daughter's fleece jacket reminds me of the character Flat Stanley, who appears in a children's book of the same name. Flat Stanley is mailed in an envelope to visit his relatives. School children mail a paper cutout of Flat Stanley to their own relations with instructions to take a picture of him in places of interest. It's a geography lesson in an envelope.

Caroline E's fleece could tell stories from California to New England, from the deep South to Europe. But the best story it could tell is of one night on its way to a restaurant on Anguilla, West Indies. My fleece and I were riding in the back seat of a rental car; my twin sister sat next to me.

My levelheaded twin turned to me and said, "We're going to a restaurant to eat, silly."

I looked at her as if she were crazy and told her I knew that already.

She looked at me and said, "Then why did you ask me where we were going?"

When I told her I hadn't and upon inquiry, no one else in the car had asked that either, we looked at each other and I knew: my fleece jacket—and Caroline E.—were both along for the ride.

VARIATION: THE FIVE-PART EXERCISE

In other bereaved mother writing groups, I have asked women to bring something belonging to their child to the all-day session. (This exercise works well in any writing group. People don't even have to bring something special. They can pick from what they're got with them—a ring or watch, their phone. Whatever attracts them.)

I tell the writers the exercise takes about fifteen minutes and that the first four sections take two minutes each. First, describe the object—what it looks like: color, texture, size—and I set a timer for two minutes.

"Now for two minutes write your feelings about the object."

Next, write similes and metaphors the object reminds them of. Sometimes I unstrap my watch and hold up it. "My watch is like a snake that has swallowed a mouse," I might say, referring to the bulge of the watch face. Or, "My watch is my boss."

In the fourth section, write from the point of view of the object. The watch might say: "Why does she dangle me before these people and talk about me? I like to be around her wrist, quietly ticking and doing my job."

Writers then read over what they've written in all four sections and spend about five minutes culling phrases they like from the sections. They then create a short ode to the object. This exercise invites a fresh look at a beloved object, a new relationship to it.

THE ART PRINT

After an intense writing prompt, like: "Write about something belonging to your child," I always follow with a less personal visual offering. Art prints can take us out of our familiar frame; they tend to encourage descriptive writing, and can provide a safe and neutral starting point. I like to offer a wide collection of art that features both familiar images and some that most people have never seen.

I placed the prints around the room on all the available surfaces, the low bookshelves, conference table, and windowsills.

"Pick whichever print speaks to you," I said. "If you want, you can pick more than one. You don't have to have a reason for your choice. Just go for what attracts you. My only request is that you not talk."

I always discourage chitchat. We do too much of it in our daily lives already, at least I do. I wanted them to focus on the task and not get distracted.

A few women saw what they wanted and claimed their prints right away. "If two people want to use the same print," I said, "sit beside each other for this exercise. You can share."

They wrote for about twenty minutes.

Julie Hester:
Edgar Degas painting "Dancers at the Old Opera House:"
I used to be a dancer. Way back when I was young. Was I ever really that comfortable in my own skin? Did I really feel free enough to move through space and time and music with grace? I feel so tight now. Closed in. Like I need to keep myself in control or I'll fly off into space. If I started to spin I might never stop.

When did I lose touch with that ability? To let go and feel music and move, instead of thinking so damn much all the time? Was it when my body let me down?

Why can't I let go of my head and let my body move? Let it feel? I think that there might be a little bit of heaven in dancers, a connection with spirit and light and joy and love.

I had a t-shirt back then that said, "To dance is to live." Because I quit dancing, does it mean I'm dead? Dead inside. If I started to dance again, would I start to thaw and maybe, one day, live again? Be able to spin and move and laugh and love and finally rest? Tired out from dancing, instead of coping?

Kelly Sechrist wrote about an art photograph of a doll among brambles.

My husband David bought two dolls, one for me and one for Abigail. They are intricately dressed with little lace hats, in smocked dresses with layers and layers of fabric. They sit in Abby's room, perched regally on doll stands, blankly staring. Their glass eyes are cold, like a frosted window. I can't reach in and I want to—to pull out my daughter. Their porcelain faces are cool to the touch, reminding me of Abby the day of the funeral. She looked like a porcelain doll dressed in her white eyelet bonnet and white gown. She was so fragile. I wanted to pick her up, return her to her warm living state—but she was surrounded by thorns and brambles. Nature had already taken her.

Unsent Letters

We began to wrap up the day, as the autumn light faded, by writing a letter to our child—or children. (Beverly Burton had lost both sons. If someone in the group has lost more than one child make sure to include the plural. Otherwise that person might feel alienated.)

Those of us old enough to have written letters in earlier decades find this a familiar, easy-to-approach form of writing. I suggested that the women might want to write a series of letters, starting with the one they wrote that afternoon, as a way of somehow keeping in touch, the way Betsy had done in her book about Caroline Elizabeth, *Fly On, My Sweet Angel.*

Dottye Currin:

Dear Alex,

I can't believe it has been so many years since you died. And if people had told me I could still take a breath this many years removed from that day, I would have doubted them.

I'm so sorry that even I did not know your heart. Not really. Not so much that I could stand up for you — that I could be as proud of you then as I am now.

So many people live their lives and fail to mean what you have meant to friends and family. At your funeral, when your friends were telling the world what kind of person you were, I was so proud. And I was so sad. Because not only did I not know how they felt, you also did not know.

How different our lives might have been if we both had known the truth —

If we'd both embraced your sweet disposition and your warm heart — If we had fought together your limitations and MY limitations.

I am so grateful to have been blessed by your spirit, to have had God's grace in learning how to accept the truth and to be truthful. You have done that for me. In your death, you have given new life to me. And so you will continue to touch people. . . .

Sometimes I feel so foolish trying to talk to you from my limited knowledge. You have a supreme knowing now. You are the teacher, the counselor, the guiding light. In partnership with a loving God who has always been with you, and with me, your spirit has guided me to be more than I could ever have been without you. I hope you are proud of me now. I hope you will continue to be with me.

Much love,

Mom

P.S. Say hello to Spanky and Corky!

We all know how to write a letter and it's often easy to get thoughts out in a conversational tone when we have a recipient in mind. The 16th century French essayist Michel de Montaigne retired from public life at age 38 to write about and explore his inner states of being. His best friend had died a few years earlier. Scholars believe that Montaigne's reflective and highly accessible *Essays* were one-way discussions with his dead friend.

WRITING BACK

As an adjunct to The Unsent Letter, I asked the women to invite their dead children to write a letter back. Note: If you haven't lost a child or someone else close to you, this prompt might strike you as odd or bizarre. But for many bereaved mothers, who talk to their children and hear their children's voices in their heads, it's an opportunity to give their children the chance to speak up on the page.

If you offer this exercise also give something else to do instead for those who may feel awkward receiving a letter. You could suggest writing a letter to someone else who was involved at the time of the child's death.

CLOSING

We closed with an open reading. Anyone could read anything they had written that day.

Then I asked them to name aloud the exercises we had done and I wrote them on the board: Lists, Before/After, Healing Place, Dialogue with Aspect of Self, Letter to Child, etc. Many people will write down what the leader writes on the board. I encourage this. It's a way to review and remember.

We went over each exercise briefly. I suggested they write on their own, using some of the prompts from the day or whatever else came to mind. "Set a timer for fifteen minutes and write," I said. "That might make the task less daunting."

I told them about how, months after Malcolm died, I had set aside an hour a day, cranked my kitchen timer, and written notes to all the people who had written to me during and after his life.

When the timer sounded, I stopped, putting away the notes and my stationery and stamps until next session. Limiting the time I spent corresponding helped me face the task. Sometimes the ink on the note cards would smear with tears and I'd have to start again. Still, I answered every note. When I sealed the last envelope, I didn't feel the sense of closure I longed for, but I did feel that I had passed some sort of important milestone. The notes were no longer burdening me. I had written them, given myself time, at regular intervals, to explore my feelings.

As I final exercise, I asked them to reflect on the day and write for five minutes about what the time together had brought them, what they might take away, and what they might want to write about later.

To-Go Prompts

At the very end, I read a poem by William Stafford called "Yes."

"I'll give you a copy of the poem," I said. "You can use it at home. I call these, 'To-Go Prompts.'"

As I handed out the poem and other materials, several women expressed interest in meeting again.

Note: I always hold handouts of any kind until the end of the workshop. Otherwise people will read them instead of writing.

"We're just getting started," Dottye said.

"Please, let's have another session," Scharme added.

I told them I'd see what I could do and that meanwhile I'd share all their contact information so they could keep in touch by email. I made a point of saying that if someone did not want to be on the email list to let me know.

Closing rituals are not exactly my thing—chimes and ceremonies and all that. But before leaving, we closed our eyes and held hands in a few moments of silence. I then passed the "Quaker squeeze," a ritual from my childhood that my family did sitting around the table before dinner.

"When you feel the squeeze," I said, "pass it on by pressing the person's hand on the other side of you. I'll let you know when the squeeze gets back to me."

Not one of us, on that fall afternoon, could have conceived that several years into our futures, we'd be planning a 10th anniversary trip to southern France—to write together for a week in a 12th century chateau.

FIVE YEARS

And so our mothers and grandmothers have, more often than not anonymously, handed on the creative spark, the seed of the flower they themselves never hoped to see—or like a sealed letter they could not plainly read.

—Alice Walker

CAROUSEL CENTER

We met for a second writing workshop in a conference room at the Carousel Center Hospice building where Diane Spaugh, pictured above (left) with Monica and me, worked. She had reserved us the space. It was a drizzly cold Saturday morning in March of 2003, five months after our initial day together. This time we would meet only for the morning, not a full day as we had before. Kelly brought her baby, Cohen, born since we'd last met. He was in a stroller that lay flat so he could sleep. And he was attached to a breathing monitor; she wasn't about to lose a second baby to SIDS.

As steady cold rain made puddles in the parking lot, I put up the Guidelines sheet from the first session and invited everyone to sit down. As I looked around me I saw grim faces, pleading eyes, tight shoulders. I set a vase of water on the large table we were sitting around and pulled from my canvas bag, fourteen daffodils wrapped in a damp paper towel and aluminum foil. I took a flower and passed the bouquet to Kelly, who was on my left, telling her to take one for Abby and pass them along.

"Who couldn't be here this morning?" Dottye asked, taking a daffodil for her son Alex.

"Peggy couldn't come," I said. "And Kathy."

"I'll take a flower for Peggy," Dottye said. "Her daughter was Rebecca, right?"

"Right," I said.

"There are two for you, Beverly," I said, when the flowers reached her.

"I'll take one for Ryan as well, since Kathy isn't here."

Kathy was not going to be with us for a while. Too much was going on in her family, she told me. Her son Wesley was required by law to offer community-service talks to groups of teenagers about the dangers of driving too fast—this while fighting survivor guilt and grieving the death of his brother and good friends. Kathy's youngest child, Mandy, twelve at the time of the accident, was struggling with major depression. The family was in therapy together and individually. But still, she wished to be included in emails and to rejoin us as soon as her life settled down and she felt less traumatized.

When the flowers had been passed around the room, I put my bright yellow daffodil in the teal blue vase. "This is for Malcolm," I said. "The bouquet can be our centerpiece this morning."

We went around the room and each woman put a flower in the bowl, naming her child as she did.

Beverly put in three flowers. "This is for Wes," she said, and put one flower in the vase. "This is for Andy," she said, putting another daffodil in the bowl. "And this one is for Kathy's Ryan."

Even though all the fluorescent overhead lights were on, the room seemed dark, cheerless, despite the bright daffodils. I had planned to have the women warm up with the prompt: "I remember," but the room seemed so jangly and tense that I felt I had to address the edgy mood immediately, not turn away from it.

"So, how do you feel right now about being here," I asked. "Start writing any time."

Some women sat and wiped their eyes; others began writing immediately; others wrote and blew their noses.

In consideration for Kelly, Barbara didn't want to read aloud what she had written, but she sent it to me afterwards:

It's an unusual instance,
Having a baby in the room.
If I am honest, I guess I'm a bit jealous.
I remember William as a baby, breastfeeding him, loving that feeling.
(I'd remember this fondly, even if he hadn't died.)
The warm, loving closeness: I miss it.
But then, that's what I miss most, the touch, the warmth, his nearness.
I hope every mother appreciates these things.
I'm sure this particular mother (Kelly) does!
I know she guards this time as precious and she knows how quickly it can be gone.
This room full of women:
I am still amazed by the hurt and the pain in this room right now.
This is not just about me: it is about ALL of us!
This common thread, this cord that connects us all.
Wonder where the day will take us.

I passed around the red bear and asked if anyone had written anything between sessions, or so far this morning, or in the last session that she'd like to share. Some women held the bear, stroked it and passed—the struggle of whether or not to read contorting their faces. Some admitted they hadn't opened their dappled composition books since our day together all those months earlier.

Dottye Currin wanted to read what she had just written:

Sisterhood. A sorority one would never choose, Fate has chosen for us. Our sons and daughters, in concert, with voices of knowing and souls of a unique and endless love, peek in to this den of expression.

Life is here. And remembering. And hope.

When we met before, we had no idea of the awesome power our collection of voices would deliver. I feel privileged. I feel at one in a way that I can find no other place.

War is looming and the world is scared. I am dismayed and distressed. But I am not afraid of dying. I wish for peace and the laying down of arms. From my seat here, I continue to seek another peace and the laying down of truth.

Julie Hester read about Ash Wednesday.

I watch as the ashes move from the clay pot to my forehead. A few fall down on my face, on my nose, onto the chancel rail where my hands are clasped in a sort of prayer.

How do you pray when you know all too well that to ashes we all return?

Ashes to ashes

Dust to dust

How do I explain to Hank and Lucy that what's behind the stone with Jack's name in The Garden is ashes? How can a child understand that a living, breathing person can become the stuff of liturgy—that stains the forehead and the heart, and is swept away but never really gone?

How can a child understand?

How can a mother?

Between sessions, I had emailed the women a poem by Louise Gluck called "Snowdrops," from a volume, *The Wild Iris*. In some of the poems in this collection, Gluck writes from the point of view of plants, here the snowdrop bulb in winter.

". . . I did not expect to survive.
in the raw wind of the new world . . ."

I reread the poem that morning. A powerful piece of poetry like this invites a writer to think in metaphor, of herself perhaps as a cold bulb, freezing all winter in dark earth. Thinking in metaphor and simile expands our worldview and, in the way that myth does, allows us to reach into archetypal truth and see how we're all part of it. Many of us have felt, at times, utterly isolated and cold and as though we're living in darkness. Identifying with the natural world can hearten a bleak vision.

"Let your minds explore," I said. "When you write, your imagination will take you to surprising places, regions you won't go when you're just thinking. New thoughts emerge on the page."

While the women's pens moved across the pages, I held Cohen. Nobody else paid much attention to the little guy.

I next invited the women to sit and reflect on their children, to watch a movie in their heads, starring their child (or children—as in Beverly's situation). I suggested they write about a gesture or a habit of their child's. Several of the women had told me, after the first session, that they liked having the time, within the safety of the group, to write about and memorialize their children in words. They wanted to release images they were holding and create written testimony, legacies to their children.

Beth Baldwin:

Bran, we could have learned so much from you if we had only stopped to listen. You had a kindness and a gentleness about you that I'm not sure we even told you how much we appreciated. You befriended the underdog and the fringe characters in high school. Some of those bestudded and tattooed personalities you brought home, draped in black and leather, were clearly absent from the school honor roll, but maybe not from the "FBI Most Wanted List"! You told us that they were good inside and that outside appearances don't count. I said I hoped you were right, because it appeared that one of my silver teaspoons had disappeared from the kitchen counter.

That's when you grew that King Tut goatee. Your dad and I tried not to say anything much about that King Tut goatee, because you told us that appearances don't count, but when it got to be eight inches long, I got mad at it one day and yelled some obscenities at it. I hope you don't think those words were directed at you; they were aimed only at that obnoxious goatee. Thank you for keeping it only six more months and for shaving it off after it became a long, totally frozen Brillo pad on our ski trip.

A time came when I thought a lot about appearances. Your gaunt skeletal body, too weak to sit up. Rosy cheeks turned to sunken ash. Hair thinning and almost absent from your face. I'd have given anything for that King Tut goatee and for the tall, healthy body that went with it. All that was left was a scarred side, arms outstretched to the morphine pump, and a final message of love and acceptance. What is the meaning in all of that?

Monica Sleap:

Katie's violin rests comfortably between the velvet in her violin case, its melody long silent since her last recital practice. She played her violin for many different people, to bring joy and harmony into their lives. Young children loved to touch and hold her violin, even trying to eke out a few notes. Katie would guide the children in the proper way to hold the instrument and the bow. The elderly in nursing homes had their otherwise quiet days lifted by her music.

Katie carried her violin case slung over one of her shoulders, bringing her six-foot height down about half an inch. Her dad and I would always remind her about her posture.

Katie brought immeasurable joy to our parents by playing solo concerts for them. She stood proudly in the church balcony during my Dad's funeral service in April 1999, playing one of his favorite tunes, "Danny Boy." We are fortunate to have a tape of Katie playing her favorite violin pieces. We listen and her melody lives on in our lives.

The women wrote about themselves in the third person. "She." "What's going on with her right now?" Looking at ourselves from the third person changes how we see ourselves, can break up old stuck patterns.

By the end of the morning, I was damp and stiff from holding baby Cohen. He had been so good, hadn't even needed changing. Maybe he sensed the sober tone in the room and didn't dare act up.

Over a lunch of turkey wraps and chips from Hospice and a huge plate of cookies from Beth, we decided to meet again in six months, this time for a weekend writing retreat. Dottye told us she thought we could use her daughter's place, Breath of Sol, in the Blue Ridge Mountains.

Breath of Sun—that sounded promising.

Over the next months as the emails flew about when to meet, what to bring etc. Dottye wrote, "We'll be celebrating our one-year anniversary as a group."

We had met twice and were already talking about our first anniversary. That felt promising.

BREATH OF SOL

Up a steep winding road in the Blue Ridge mountains, we turned right at the rough-hewn sign, "Breath of Sol," carved from a tree slab. Coincidentally it included a sun with thirteen rays, one for each of us. The afternoon light was still a brilliant yellow-orange in the treetops and the sky densely blue beyond.

A retreat of any kind—sharing living space with others, if only for a weekend—is such an intimate experience, and yet we barely knew each other. But we were pulled together by a special force, a backdrop of loss. Already we were discovering that we could appreciate each other without having a lot of shared experience or background. Because of our bond, we began to feel we were forging a path together toward something new. And it was over this weekend that we first were able to laugh fully. Comic relief, irony, and dark humor—we could express these together, with surprising freedom, and everyone in the group seemed to have a good sense of humor. We lucked out on that front.

Many of us came straight from work or a house full of young children, or both or neither. Barbara wasn't able to attend. Kathy was still taking time off from the group. And Kelly, who was nursing Cohen, couldn't get away. This was probably for the best: the group wasn't yet ready to host a baby—for a weekend. Besides, Kelly also had a toddler at home.

The women now talk about how reluctant they had been to drive to the mountains together and so didn't. "No way was I going to travel with anybody," Monica said. "I mean, I didn't even know these people."

Dottye's A-frame had three bedrooms on the lowest floor and another on the top. The middle floor held a large fireplace in the communal living dining area and a good-sized kitchen. The back wall was entirely glass, opening onto a deck overlooking the woods and mountains. This floor offered a snug gathering place for a group our size.

We decided then and there that we were through with chilly boardrooms, fluorescent lighting, and stiff chairs.

"I'm going to keep the fire roaring all weekend," Dottye told us, adding that she planned to sleep on the living room couch.

"You can be Hestia," I said, "goddess of the hearth and home."

"Great," she said. "And this way I won't have to share a bedroom with anybody. Plus I'm kind of deaf so once I take out my hearing aids nobody will keep me up at night—even if you bang pots and pans around in the kitchen to scare away bears! And," she added, smiling. "Walt tells me I snore. Like he should talk!"

Betsy and Kay knew each other a bit better than the rest of us so they decided to share the master bedroom upstairs. Kay was teaching high school English all week and spending every Saturday running errands and caring for her elderly mother. She also traveled to the coast to care for her grandchildren, or sometimes hosted them at her house, four hours from the shore. For her, going away for a weekend and giving undivided attention to her own life was a rare treat.

Kay told us she had not cleared out Elizabeth's room. She later wrote:

Miss Havisham, the character from Charles Dickens' Great Expectations, has been in the back (or front) of my mind for a long time . . . Miss Havisham (have-a-sham) is the character who was jilted on her wedding day. She stopped all the clocks in the house when she heard the news. She wore her wedding gown, and one shoe on and one off, for twenty years and left her surroundings frozen in time—including the rotting wedding cake.

So much of Elizabeth's room has not been dismantled or put away in the ten years since she died that I hear a thin echo of Miss Havisham's life in mine. . . I thought I really let Miss H. go last year, the last time I taught the novel. But she is larger than life and always will be. Miss H. had hurt others by her monomania. I hope I haven't hurt anyone by neglecting to put away Elizabeth's things. Her room has been transformed into the play area of choice for Anna, Sara and Maria, my granddaughters, her nieces.

During one recent visit, Anna said that it was so nice of Aunt Elizabeth to leave all of her toys for them to play with.

So how and why does Miss Havisham still haunt me? Is it that I've simply stopped time in that room? I don't think so. Is it that I've refused to acknowledge that a tragedy really did stop my life as it was? Maybe. But I think I've done a good deal of growing and healing in the last ten years. I think I've compartmentalized the Miss Havisham part.

When I went into Elizabeth's room after the accident, I found jeans wadded on the floor along with other piles of clothing, and I washed them all, as if she were coming back. I didn't just leave the room in Miss Havisham fashion, exactly as it was. I cleaned up a little. I made her bed, and months later, her brother Matt sat on that bed and wept, finding Elizabeth's long blonde hairs still on the pillow.

And that doll house. Her brother Aaron and I put it together the Christmas she was six. Gradually she painted and wallpapered the tiny rooms, and every time we went to the orthodontist, her reward was a visit to Miss Muffet's for more dollhouse furnishings. Just a few weeks before she died, Liz and some teenaged friends who stayed overnight, rearranged furniture and the tiny place settings.

My granddaughter Anna has loved that doll house for at least three years. Sara and Maria enjoy it too. They hide the tiny cups and saucers and fake food in corners of the room, the way Elizabeth did. I don't know if I'll ever get it all back together, or if I need to.

I found tiny Guatemalan "worry dolls" made from wire and scraps of fabric that Elizabeth hid in sand castle sculptures when we went to the beach and among the books on her bedroom shelves, signs of how my daughter let her worries go before she went to sleep at night. And years later as I sold little bags of "worry dolls" to nine-year-olds at Christmas at the Fair Trade mission shop, I smiled every time, thinking of my own girl and her sweet ways.

We settled into the cabin with our bags and writing materials. Peggy and I had agreed to be roommates.

"Mike says I snore," Peggy told me, "but I won't have to hear it."

"Great," I said. "Thanks for the heads-up."

Another possible snag: There was only one bed. We decided we could share it.

"I'll be fine as long as I can have the far side," Peggy said. "That way my deaf ear can be up and I won't hear you in the night."

"But what about me? I don't have a deaf ear."

"Sorry," she said and shrugged. "Got ear plugs?"

Beverly called to us from the other room. "Stop quibbling, you two. You sound like an old married couple."

Piling into the house produced the sensation that we were all girlfriends at a college reunion. But, of course, we weren't. Though we understood aspects of each other deeply through our writing, in other ways, we were hardly acquainted. We were from different generations, for one thing. And we weren't there to reminisce, get tipsy, talk about how much, or how little, our lives had altered over the years.

As I watched four of the women—Julie, Beverly, Monica, and Scharme—stow their bags away and test the four narrow beds in their dormitory-type room, I admired their brio. To be here, to share rooms, to commit to a weekend of writing with women they barely knew, and about such a difficult subject, this would not be easy.

Many of the women arrived dressed nicely in outfits from Chico's or Anne Taylor. They wore make-up, belted slacks, and neatly ironed blouses. But the minute we all tumbled into this quaint, if a bit moldy, cabin all the make-up came off. Everybody changed into sweats, yoga tops, and slippers, and gathered in the living room around the blazing fire. There was no need to look put-together here; we could relax–even though, years later, several women recalled the terror they had felt at the start of the weekend, with its close sleeping quarters and lack of privacy.

Beth was the last to arrive. We gave her the free room downstairs. It had a double bed, but the walls and even the pillowcases were damp. Not ideal, but at least she wouldn't have to share a bed or even a room.

"I can sleep well on a rock," Beth had said before the weekend. With her slim frame and tidy clothes this seemed incongruous. But when I showed her the room, she smiled. "This is like the Ritz compared to some places I've slept," she said. "Trust me."

Peggy had draped a piece of black cloth on a side table in the living room. On it, we displayed items of value from our children's lives. Together they created a collective weekend shrine:

Julie: the hand-knit white baby cap with a blue stripe and a picture of baby Jack in the hospital, tubes protruding from his tiny body.

Beth: stones, including quartz. Branner had been a rock climber and collector.

Peggy: a candle holder with some of Rebecca's items–earrings, rings, hair clips–embedded in it.

Beverly: Wes's license plate, and a handmade map of a golf course Andy had designed.

Kay: a branch of ginkgo leaves (Elizabeth loved their heart shape), a photo of Elizabeth, and a small pile of her daughter's favorite childhood books.

Monica: pictures of the roadside shrine at Katie's accident site and a necklace with a penguin charm, Katie's favorite animal.

Betsy: Caroline Elizabeth's pink baby blanket.

Scharme: a photo of one of Steve's dogs and pictures from a trip she and Steve took out west.

Dottye: family pictures, including one of Alex in uniform.

I added a picture of Malcolm and me in the first hospital, when I was tan and he was pink-cheeked, before we knew anything was wrong.

Like most women getting together for a weekend away, we brought enough food to feed a small country for a day or two. Casseroles, baked chickens, bowls of salads—bean, potato, mixed green—cheeses, cold cuts, hummus, bottles of wine, yogurt, and eggs stuffed the refrigerator shelves. Breads, bagels, crackers, trail mix, cakes, and pies lined the counters.

We had made a schedule of who would cover which meals. Performing those daily, familiar chores—chopping, heating up casseroles, setting the table, finding glasses and plates in the cupboard—all these routine tasks helped everyone relax in each other's company that first night. Later Monica said that eating dinner together felt like a form of communion. When we finally sat down to our first meal prepared by us, a hush came over the group.

"Julie, you're the minister," Dottye said. "Say something."

"Hey, I'm off duty," Julie said. But she offered a brief blessing and we dug in. Before dessert, the house phone rang, startling us with its jarring peal. Dottye had given out the number for emergencies since many of our cell phones didn't get reception up there in the mountains.

"It could be important," Monica said.

"Or it could be a sales call," Dottye added. "Let's hope it's a vacuum cleaner promotion."

No one wanted to answer it. Many of us had a history with calls like this, of receiving devastating news by way of the telephone. Dottye picked up the receiver, hoping to hang up on a telemarketer.

It was Beth's husband Sandy.

"I need to talk to him," Beth said, pushing back from the table. She went to a corner of the front room and talked in a hushed tone.

When she came back, she confessed. "On the way up here, I got a speeding ticket. I called Sandy and told him to contact our attorney."

"Unreal," somebody said. "I got pulled too, but just got a warning."

"Me too," Julie said.

We figured it had probably been the same zealous state trooper each time. Being the last to arrive, Beth was the unlucky one: the trooper must have decided he'd been forgiving enough.

"Sandy went to the club this afternoon and everybody was asking where I was," Beth said. "He told them I'd gone away for the weekend—to *a grief writing contest.*"

"You're kidding," Monica said, her expression stoical as always. "A grief writing *contest?*"

I looked around the candlelit table and saw that every face was smiling. Bright eyes reflected the flames.

"*Of course* my husband would see this as some sort of competition. He's Mr. Spreadsheet and Mr. Golf Score."

"Maybe we *should* have a grief writing contest," Monica said, and when we all laughed, added, "Really. I mean it."

"Well, okay," I said. "You're on. Whoever types up and emails me the most of her journal entries wins."

We had already decided to compile pieces of our writing in some form. At least the contest would be incentive to get words from the journals into the computers.

"Will there be a prize?" Monica asked, "for whoever sends the most writing?"

"Maybe," I said.

"And what will it be?" she asked. "An extra writing prompt for the winner? Some prize."

They were already teasing me for making them write—a lot.

Monica Sleap:

My husband Rick and I agree that letting our parents know about Katie's death was the most difficult part of her passing from this life. We had to tell them that on her way to school that morning, approximately two miles from our house, Katie's car slid on ice into the path of a van traveling in the opposite direction. Despite emergency medical assistance, Katie died a short time later.

Arriving home from the hospital that afternoon with our other daughter Jenn, we saw Katie's newly washed jeans and tops drying where she'd left them that morning. Her prized penguin T-shirt hung from a hook in the kitchen, where it still hangs today.

Most gatherings of women function well, and this group was no exception. A self-selected core took over the kitchen and got the meal together. Others cleaned up. Women just know how to do things, how to divvy up tasks. Without having to discuss who does what, women manage to get it all done without a lot of fuss.

After dinner we sat around the fire for an opening exercise I call a body check. I asked the women to relax and sit comfortably. I suggested they note where they felt tightness in their bodies, starting with their toes and working up. Where were they holding pain, grief, tension?

"Try to be aware of these places all weekend and send warmth and light to these areas."

We also wrote that night about what mattered, at that exact moment, there in the mountain cabin.

And we made self-care lists. Here's part of mine.

For Self Care:
- *Journaling.*
- *Early-morning solitude watching the dawn, writing down my dreams.*
- *Lying on the living room couch staring out the window—"drool time."*
- *Epsom salts baths. "The salts draw toxins from the body," Mother says.*
- *Walking the dog in the woods (after snake season).*
- *Listening to books on CD in the car makes driving bearable.*

As it turns out, I had brought ear plugs (my husband snores) but Peggy's breathing wasn't nearly as bad as something else she hadn't told me about: her restless leg syndrome. One of her calves twitched and jumped all night. In the morning, I made sure to tell her.

"Well, you exhaled in little puffs," she said, "And that bugged me."

"You heard that with your deaf ear?"

"I guess I'm not completely deaf. Good to know."

We spent the weekend writing around the crackling fire in the living room and outdoors, sitting on tree stumps and rocks in the sharp autumn air. We took leisurely walks, in groups or alone, and gathered around the large table for meals.

Before a weekend retreat, I always send a story or book or poem for everyone to read in advance. Having a common text to refer to, especially in the early meetings, helps build community and offers a perspective from an outside source—it can be easier to respond to than personal material.

Following up on our earlier writing about a child's gesture, I had them write about the Raymond Carver story, "A Good Small Thing."

The story contains a stunning gesture–the father cradles his dead son's bicycle wheel.

Over dinner Saturday night we talked about Robert Frost and all the losses he had endured: several young children, an adult son to suicide, a wife to madness. I read his poem, "Never Again Would Birds' Song Be the Same," written after his adult daughter died. Through birdcalls he kept her close; for him his daughter lived on in their song.

After dinner our prompt was: how we keep our children close.

Many of the women wrote about their other children and grandchildren, and how they saw aspects of their dead children in their living. I watched Beverly closely. Both of her children were gone. She couldn't look forward to grandchildren, didn't have any children to enjoy. Later that night we sat out on the back deck watching the stars. I asked Beverly to join me on the steps, away from the others. We talked quietly. Everyone in the group appreciated our common bonds of loss, but she was the only one of us who had lost all of her children.

"Do you feel 'other' within our group?"

"No," she said, wrapping her arms around her knees and looking me right in the eye. "I've experienced so much loss over the past few years–my mother, sister-in-law, mother-in-law, my teenage sons. I don't know what I'd do if I didn't have an abiding faith in God. That keeps me from feeling 'other.'"

I mentioned an essay called "Is Theology Poetry?" by C. S. Lewis, and paraphrased his thoughts on faith. He writes: "I believe in Christianity as I believe that the sun has risen. Not only because I see it, but because by it I see everything else."

"Amen, sister," she said. "That's how I feel."

The many ways people fill the gaping holes reflect the vastness of human differences. Beverly told me she enjoyed spending time with her boys' friends, leading them in church retreats, having them to supper. Other women in our group couldn't bear events involving their dead children's friends—the graduations, weddings, and baby showers.

"I'll let you know," Beverly said quietly, "if I ever feel alienated."

On Sunday morning the women wrote short tributes to their

children. I decided to share something my husband had written for the memorial service we had for Malcolm in the vast chapel where we'd been married seven years before he was born. As I read Bill's words in the cozy A-frame, surrounded by this group of mothers, I felt my insides begin to shake, and not in the Pilates "feel-the-core" sort of way. A weakness moved through my bones and something grabbed at my lungs.

. . .*He had a lanky, well-formed body, with big feet, like his grandfather's, that might someday have carried him down a cinder track. And aside from his fatal defect, he was tough and resilient. And this is very hard: that the life he would have grown into is now only speculation and mystery.* . .

Damn, I thought, I'm going to cry. I choked up, had to stop, and could barely eke out the words. I was the farthest in time from the death of my child, Malcolm having died in 1982. But feelings can surface, when we least expect them, as I always caution others in writing groups. Still, I was the leader and was supposed to be—what? Immune? Above it? Beyond grief?

By the time we left that afternoon, we had decided to meet at Peggy's house in Raleigh in the spring. We knew now that in spite of the pain and loss we all felt and wrote about, we were somehow at ease together. There was room for fun, a few jokes, irony—after all, we were seriously planning a grief writing contest. We had discovered that weekend that we laughed together almost as easily as we cried.

What we didn't know was that Peggy would suffer two heart attacks in January. Ironically, she had written about her heart as the place in her body where she held grief. Sitting around the blazing fire, she wrote: "*My heart had been big like a balloon but, when Rebecca died, it burst and deflated.*"

Heading down the mountain after the retreat, I called Bill and learned that my mother-in-law, who lived in an assisted living center in our town, had fallen on Friday evening at dinner and broken her knee.

"Thank you for not calling to tell me," I said. Nancy suffered from congestive heart failure and severe dementia. I was her primary care giver and would have grappled with leaving the retreat early but, he assured me, there really wasn't much I could have done.

Bill and his mother had spent all of Friday night in the ER, waiting to get her admitted.

"She screamed in pain for seven hours straight," he told me.

"Give me a grief writing contest any day over a mother-in-law yelling all night in the ER," I later emailed the women.

Peggy too had in-law concerns on her return. She emailed the group:

I got a call from my father-in-law's nursing home. He had fallen, and they were taking him to the ER to check him out. This is the same ER where they took Rebecca, even though we all pretty much figured she would not be revived.

Self care #1. I took a whole tablet of Xanax before heading to the hospital to see Dad. It did the trick and I was grateful. But after three hours of sitting in the general waiting area, when we finally were taken to a little room to meet with the doctor, my strength was waning. He said it might be two hours before they could run tests and do x-rays.

Self care #2. I absolutely hate to do this...but I told him...could he please hurry up somehow, that my daughter had died there, and of course with those words I lost my nice composure. I told him I was going home for more Xanax. He gave me the hospital phone number and said to take all the time I needed. They would care for him. But my poor old father-in-law—I was the only family he had. My husband Mike was away.

Self care #3. And this is always hard; I asked for help. I went home and at 8 p.m. went crying to my neighbor and asked if she could come back with me to the hospital; distraction works wonders, I know that, but I hate to bother someone at that hour. I knew she would come without hesitation and she stayed with me till 11 p.m. when they released Dad back to the nursing home. My neighbor's husband drove him back and found an all-night pharmacy to get pain meds filled. I got home after 12:30.

Having the self-care writing activity from the first night of the retreat so fresh in my mind enabled me to call on my neighbors. I would have spiraled into gloom alone, even WITH Xanax. But still...it IS hard to ask for help...partly because of having to first expose my vulnerability and partly because I still want to think I can handle things myself (What a dork! haha).

Monica emailed me that one of the best moments of the weekend had been my quivering voice when I read about Malcolm. "*It was at that point I realized that you really were part of our group," she wrote," that you too had really 'been there.'"*

"*No offense,*" she added, "*but your meltdown was the weekend highlight for me. Just Kidding.*"

Another email that circulated after our first retreat weekend came from Julie. She worked in children's ministry and her husband Dan was a Methodist minister:

I have to tell you all that during the retreat, on the phone, my husband asked if I was having to be a pastor to anyone. I replied, "No more so than anyone else is." So as an ordained one in the midst of the group, let me affirm the way the group was able to be priests for one another then, and will, I trust, continue to do so. Even the "pagan" ones among us! (Carol's word choice, not mine!)

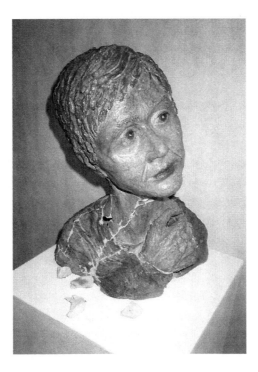

OVERNIGHT

I met with Peggy at her spacious home in Raleigh and reported to the group that she had plenty of space for writing and plenty of bedrooms and beds. Peggy had told me she wanted to do a few easy art projects with us and she showed me her large upstairs studio.

Then I got an email from Peggy's daughter Julie informing me that Peggy had had a heart attack while visiting her but that the damage was less than expected and that the doctors had put in a stent. Her long-term prognosis was good.

Peggy emailed me:

I am still eager to have the writing group meet at my house. I will have my cleaning people here beforehand, and can't see that I would have to do anything more. . .

The doctors have taken me off my ADD meds at least temporarily and that's making me crazy or more aptly a blundering idiot.
It is so good to be home.

She suffered a second heart attack but still wanted us to come. I wrote the group:

Peggy is looking forward to the chance to write and to having us there. She doesn't feel she'll have to "host" since we'll be bringing the food and our own sheets, etc. She knows she can excuse herself at any time to rest, if need be. She told me, "Having all of you isn't like having the garden club or something—not that I'd EVER be in a garden club. But I won't have to do anything."

Apparently she'd had a bad reaction to the first stent material—this happens rarely but it seemed to with her. So the doctors put another kind in, an older brand that they think will work better.

So, let's stick with our original plan and head to Raleigh.

Caring for Peggy was the unspoken theme of this retreat. Her heart problems had reminded us that mortality wasn't just in the past; the possibility of it was here and now. This time, the picture was complicated by the fact that two who came had missed the Breath of Sol meeting. Barbara remembers now that, as she set off for Raleigh, she couldn't even figure out which woman Peggy was. Kelly wasn't sure either.

"Even though so many of us were coming from the same basic area we didn't drive together," Barbara said, mirroring Monica's thoughts before the last retreat. "The thought of spending hours in the car with one of the women freaked me out. I mean I had no idea what I would talk to anybody about on a long car trip. I had completely blanked out the first meeting and all the women were still kind of a blur in my mind."

We arrived in time for lunch on Saturday with lots of hugs for Peggy and a basket of goodies from Dottye, who couldn't be with us. I had again brought a daffodil for each child; each of us put a flower into a large clear vase. Beverly again put in two for her sons and one for Kathy's son Ryan. In Dottye's absence, I put one in for Alex.

After an opening prompt, "What's going on?" we made clusters (mind maps). I suggested that everyone write down a significant adjective, or their name, in the center of a blank page, circle it, and add thoughts, as they came up, in little circled "thought bubbles" clustered around the word.

I wrote the word "overwhelmed" in the center of a blank page and circled it. I drew a line out from the central word, wrote "job," and circled it. Bubbles from job: Fall Conference, Weekly Workshops, Summer Programs, Reading Series. Each of these spawned more words. I was also offering my own writing workshops at my house, as well as a weekly class at a local art center. Each of these got its own bubble, spun off of "overwhelmed."

Our younger daughter, Colette, a junior in high school, rated a bubble. She would call me at work most afternoons and ask, "When are you coming home?" Another bubble: "Latch-key kid." I remembered coming home to an empty house when I was growing up. A key-kid myself, I didn't want this for my own children. We both needed that precious after-school time when she and I sorted through her day together.

Filling in and circling another bubble "sleep," something I wasn't getting enough of, I looked over at Peggy, perched on the edge of a couch. Her face was pale as school glue, her brown eyes dull, the darting sparkle in them gone. I knew that napping and daydreaming had filled Peggy's life over the past month. "I don't even have the energy to draw," she'd told me on the phone.

"Take a look at your cluster," I told the group, "and pick a bubble that jumps out at you. Write about it."

I jotted on my list of prompts: "Nix art project tonight—Peggy too tired." I took a glimpse at my cluster. The word "library" jumped out and I began:

I used to be able to take my mother-in-law out for a cup of late-afternoon coffee or a vodka martini. I went along with her perception, as we sat across from each other, that we were best friends from college out for a good time. She also decided I was Italian. But Nancy couldn't hear or follow anything I said anymore. Anyone unfortunate enough to sit at a table near us would have heard me shouting: "Are you enjoying Flannery O'Connor's letters?" "Hmm?" "The letters, you know your library book?" "What?" "Never mind. Good coffee, isn't it?"

I took out a fresh piece of computer paper and started another cluster, with an upcoming workshop in the center. Do I think in clusters? Maybe I always have, but I certainly do now. I make them all the time. I use them to plan essays, client meetings, book chapters. For me a cluster is like a list or an outline, only better, because there's no hierarchy of lines. Ideas spread all over a page. Each is a thought with equal weight that, later, can be color-coded or highlighted or used as the central word in another cluster.

Unease and concern for Peggy underlaid the gathering. Monica and Barbara, our two nurses, tracked her closely all afternoon. We made her sit down while we fussed around in her kitchen, preparing dinner. We gathered in the den, wrote about the words "Never" and "Forever," and turned in early.

Monica:

This prompt carried great meaning to me from the moment Carol assigned it. As I sat one day pulling thoughts together, words started to flow in a poetic verse. The final two lines are etched on Katie's gravestone along with a violin and a penguin.

. . .Never will I lose the hope that I'll see you, my friend.
Forever you're a part of me until we meet again.

Peggy and I again shared a bed, this time in the master suite off the kitchen. I woke up around 2 a.m. and saw the bathroom light on, the other side of the giant bed empty. I padded over and listened outside the door. Silence. I knocked lightly. "Peggy?"

No answer. I wondered which rooms Monica and Barbara were in upstairs, cursing myself for not paying closer attention to the sleeping arrangements. Images of Peggy lying unconscious on the bathroom floor flooded my no-longer-sleepy brain.

I called again, knocked again, then sucked in a breath and opened the bathroom door. The room was empty. Sigh. Relief. But where was Peggy? I ran out of the bedroom and up the back staircase two steps at a time, toward a light at the top. And there she was, leaning over a large table in her studio, drawing.

"I couldn't sleep," she said. "But at least I felt like drawing again. That's good."

"Well, geez," I said, exhaling loudly. "You about gave ME a heart attack."

Peggy looked drawn; she was not her normal chatty self. I decided to keep our work to a minimum in the day ahead, and to wrap things up early.

The next morning I read from Barbara Carlson's "Imperfection." In the poem, she makes an evocative list of her imperfections. The poem ends with the poet saying she'd "rather waste time listening to the rain or…. learning to purr" from her cat.

Possible Prompts, in response to the poem:

"I am falling in love with . . ."

"I am learning to love . . ."

"I am learning to fail to . . ."

We wrote about trying to love our imperfections.

I reminded them that they don't have to use complete sentences, that lists are fine ways to cover a lot of information and can also show a lot. In *The Things They Carried*, a novel about the Vietnam war, author Tim O'Brien reveals the character of each soldier in the unit by listing what they carry in their backpacks: foot powder, condoms, dope, a New Testament, a machete.

Francine Prose, in *Reading Like a Writer*, gives an example of how character can be revealed quickly through what a character is carrying. In the Paul Bowles story, "A Distant Episode," the protagonist, known as "the Professor," carries two small overnight bags full of "maps, sun lotions, and medicines." Think about what a different sense of the character we'd get if he carried not two small overnight bags but a backpack holding a flask, a journal, and a watercolor set.

Before lunch I read two pages from *The Things They Carried*. We wrote about what we carry.

Julie:

I carry Jack's footprints and picture in my wallet, though I don't take them out to look at them much anymore. Still, knowing they're there is comforting, I guess. Those tiny feet, rubbing up against insurance cards, coffee cards, discount cards to Subway, and the underwear outlet, business cards from doctors and stores where no one knows about the little boy with the tiny feet, whose picture shares a space in my wallet with their own information.

Shouldn't there be a separate place to carry Jack? Something lined with silk, padded and tied up with a special cord, like a wrapped valuable, a fine piece of jewelry or art, protected from sticky fingers, scrambling for an old receipt or a dry-cleaning ticket, flipping past him in search of whatever seems more important at the time—what must be found to go about the business of living, of errands, of a modern existence. Does he belong there among the slips of paper that tell about me?

I have Blue Cross Blue Shield insurance.

I buy books and coffee at Barnes and Noble.

I will get free underwear from L'eggs Hanes Mill Bali if I buy a few more first.

I eat Subway but forget to put the stamps on the card.

I check out books in two different counties.

I vote Democratic.

I have the number of someone named Marvin written on the back of a Stride Rite receipt.

I have a visual progression of loved ones: a husband with a dog, a fair-haired boy growing from toddler to Cub Scout, and a dark-haired girl with her books. And a baby who won't grow up. The tiny footprints of a child mixed in among the other bits of information.

If you found my wallet, forgotten, somewhere, what could you tell about me, really? Could you know my heart, from the things I carry?

Beverly:
What I Carry

I carry my head high, my shoulders back, my spine straight. I carry pride and resilience, hope and faith. I also carry an aching neck, tired shoulders, and a weary back. I carry sorrow and guilt, bewilderment and unanswered questions. I carry memories of my sons, Wes and Andy, that crouch behind every nook and turn of my day, my surroundings, my life. But, I fail to write them down. I tell myself, "Who will read them? No one really cares but Blaine and me. There's no one to pass them on to."

I also carry visions of the future—of sitting alone in a wheelchair, staring at a smudged, dirty window with aluminum blinds slicing through the world beyond, the pungent smell of urine stinging my nostrils.

But, when I carry this vision, my pride and resilience, my hope and faith say, "No Beverly, that will not be you. You will not be carried to an old person's home to rot. You will carry yourself to a little white cottage surrounded by daisies and phlox and roses and forget-me-nots. You will hire a caregiver and she will carry you to the yard where you will carry her away to another time and place by the stories of your rambunctious, wondrous boys. You will make her smile…and laugh…and cry. She will carry your stories to her family, even after your ashes have been carried away to their final resting place and your soul is carried on the wings of angels to your Wes and Andy.

We planned to meet again, in the fall at Beth's mountain house in Roaring Gap, North Carolina. We all hugged Peggy, relieved that she seemed okay, and knowing she would crash after we left. We sent Barbara home with our high hopes for the ovarian cyst surgery she was having that week.

A few days later, an email arrived from Barbara:

I did, in fact, have my ovaries removed Wednesday and all has gone extremely well—I was actually able to leave the hospital within six hours of surgery! Pathology reports come back Monday—I'll let you know.

William was there with me, from his initials printed on my order sheet—a mistake?—to the pre-op room (#27-his birthday is 2/7)—to the warm blanket they immediately gave me on arrival (he loved his blankets warmed in the dryer)—to the Rugrats music that suddenly turned on in the next room (we always watched together). I hoped we'd meet while I was in never-never land of anesthesia, but alas, it wasn't to be.

Anyway, thanks for all your thoughts and prayers. I'll let you know next week how everything turned out.

And then, a welcome follow-up:

The report is good—absolutely benign. It seems my body was producing pregnancy hormones—odd since it's been without a uterus for ten years. . . .

My heart was with Beverly and Kathy yesterday (the anniversary of their sons' deaths), as I'm sure everyone's was—I hope they feel our love—and that of their sons—I'm sure they do.

It's a sad, rainy day. Let's all get under the covers early tonight.

ROARING GAP

Beth's invitation to her exclusive enclave, Roaring Gap, was a sign that, as for her commitment to the group, she was "all in." I had not been sure about this. Beth always made suggestions for socially constructive prompts. "What are you doing to honor your child's memory," etc. but I sensed she was frustrated with the group for not being more service-driven. When she invited us to her second home, I realized she appreciated the writing process even if we weren't as product-oriented as I suspected (perhaps erroneously) she wanted us to be. She truly felt a part of the group. And perhaps that the group was an intimate and essential part of her.

Another milestone: Kathy Shoaf rejoined us that weekend, and she would bring news from Beverly, who couldn't be there—a thoughtful and generous act on Beverly's part. Surely she knew how tentative Kathy must have felt; to bring a message would give her a specific role.

Others had to miss the weekend as well—Kelly, Monica, Scharme, and Barbara. In fact, we were all busy people and knew it would be a rare session when we'd all be able to attend.

Peggy and I drove together. As we climbed into the Blue Ridge Mountains northwest of Winston-Salem, the fog thickened to the point where I could only see a few feet in front of the car. I stared hard at the double yellow line dividing the up and down lanes. Sensing a steep drop off to our left, just beyond the pavement, I hugged the curving road. A mountain seemed to rise up on the passenger side beyond Peggy. Where was the tiny post office, a key landmark in our directions?

"Wait," Peggy said, "the directions say if we start down the mountain we've gone too far."

We were definitely heading down a mountain.

Eventually, we found our way. Beth, Kathy and Kay drifted in behind us—materializing out of the fog like ghosts. The house was perfect. Off a long interior hall were five bedrooms divided by a central staircase leading down to a large open living and dining area, the kitchen, and a sunroom. We settled into Beth's living room, its wall of windows offering (we imagined) a spectacular view on a clear day. All we could see was gray and the occasional hint of a dark hedge at the end of the sloping lawn.

The first order of business was to welcome Kathy back to the group.

"It's my birthday today," she said. "I can't imagine a better present than being back with you all." Despite the tragedy she had endured, Kathy had a bright girlish voice, a ready laugh, and a perky interest in everything.

We unpacked food in the kitchen, groaning at the trail mix and M&M's Beth always put out at our meetings although she, unlike the rest of us, rarely sampled.

Kathy dipped her hand into a bowl of treats. "Forget my diet. This weekend is a gift I'm giving myself and my family is giving me."

"And you're giving to all of us," Kay added. "We're so glad to have you back."

"It's Dan's birthday too," Julie said, her mouth twisted into an almost smirk. "And guess what? I left him at home with our two little kids! It's a gift for him to have me here with all of you, here where I feel sane."

Beverly, who hadn't missed a session until now, was chaperoning a church youth retreat that included Kathy's daughter Mandy. "I signed up to chaperone ages ago, before I knew about the writing weekend plans," she told me. I wondered if Beverly's absence might have made coming back a bit easier for Kathy. I wasn't sure and didn't ask. The two women were still friends, though they didn't see each other as often as they once had.

As we were getting out journals and pens, readying to write to the first prompt, Kathy announced she had brought news.

"I just have to tell you all now," she said. "Is that okay?" She looked at me.

"Please," Peggy said. "We'll do anything to avoid writing."

"You can say that again," Dottye added.

I tried to give them the stony-teacher look but they both just laughed.

"Okay, Kathy," I said. "Let's hear your news first."

Kathy began, her voice shaky and high. "Beverly and Blaine have decided to adopt a baby girl. From China. Beverly wanted me to tell you. And she already has a name. Hope."

We were all silent for a moment, before erupting into cheers— and tears.

"What a prompt," I said. "Let's start by writing about this news."

The room became so quiet we could almost hear the fog curling outside. Baby Hope might not have even been born yet but she already had twelve doting godmothers eagerly waiting to meet her.

That night at Roaring Gap, we wrote to the prompt: I remember . . . This is an excellent prompt to use any time to jump-start memory.

Dottye:

In that first gathering of mothers who had experienced a crisis of magnificent proportions, what all mothers secretly dread: the death of a child, there was no way to know what might happen. My greatest fear was that I might, through introspection and writing, discover truths about myself that I did not want to face. I showed up thinking that if the day seemed too emotionally draining I would just pack my things and go home.

I also planned to leave if, as I anticipated, I was not able to gather my thoughts or even think of anything to write. I am NOT a writer, so I wasn't even afraid of having "writer's block." I just didn't want to embarrass myself by not being able to participate in this "writing" workshop.

The one thing in my favor was that Salem College is my alma mater. I love Salem and feel a special connection with the history and the place. I had spent four years on the campus and usually felt very much at home. On that morning, on the third floor of the library, I felt loneliness, concern, anticipation, and a morsel of hope.

Now I remember, as I hear these others tell how they felt, then and now. I remember the gut-wrenching sorrow. I remember my waking thought for so many months, "Alex is dead." I remember the guilt about not being there for him, the anger that NO ONE was there for him.

Yet the peace in knowing that God was there, that God was saying, "You have been a good steward, you can come with me now; I am here with you and I will hold tight to you."

Alex, sitting in that cold car in that harsh, ice-covered parking lot, listening to music his friend had recorded for him, a few favorite songs to enjoy on the Naval ship. In these last minutes of life, playing the music so loudly as if to block out the demons and the shrill voices of damnation.

I remember the fear: how could I possibly comfort Karin, his younger sister, who had been wailing for days? And how can I reach Glenn? Will he ever talk about his feelings? Just a few days earlier, Glenn and Alex had been wrestling and rolling all over the floor in Glenn's room. Once again, as I had done so many times before, I went up and told them to "chill!" I was afraid they would hurt each other. Little did I know what the real hurt would be. And soon.

The fog was gone in the morning, opening the view to a vast valley punctuated by a distinct mountain in the middle and a range at the horizon. Towns dotted the rolling green hills below. Betsy offered an early-morning stretch class. A few sleepy women showed up, including me.

"If this is stretching, what's exercising?" somebody asked, panting at the rigorous progression of crunches and push-ups. The next morning she did her workout by herself, and that was fine. We all take care of ourselves in the group. It's clear that no one is obliged to participate in the peripheral activities—walks, stretching, or late-night games and chats. Attendance is required only for the writing sessions, and no one has to read (though everyone usually does).

We often start a significant chunk of writing time with a "check-in" prompt. After breakfast, I'll give one of what I call my preposition prompts: "What's behind me?" Or "What's under me?" "What's above?" "What's inside me?" "Beyond me?" Just about every preposition works well.

After warming up that Saturday morning, I read a poem, "I Used to Be But Now I'm" by Ted Berrigan and invited the women to use this opening line as a refrain in their writing. "Start every line with it," I suggested. Kay commented that this exercise reminded her of our first workshop when we wrote about "before and after" our children's deaths. "We all used to be people that we aren't anymore," she said.

That weekend we wrote from a surviving sibling's point of view. I would not have given this prompt had Beverly (who, remember, had no surviving children) been there. We all found this exercise difficult even though the subject was one we'd thought so much about—our other children's feelings.

There is no way to protect children from grief, and from the loss they live with, over the deaths of their siblings. My daughters hadn't even been born when their older brother died, but they have still been affected, deeply, by his too-short life. Their own family experience has taught them that children die. Also, they are living examples of the fact that such a death alters the playing field: had their brother lived, they wouldn't be here. These realizations have lasting emotional consequences. For bereaved mothers, tending to our living children is another huge burden. Witnessing their grief over the loss of a sibling often leaves us feeling hideously inadequate. We can't fix their pain and our own often threatens to drown us.

Betsy:

Michael's Music

With apologies to Michael, I share this insight into a mistake I made in the first few weeks after Elizabeth died. I don't really know what was going on inside my son's head when this particular incident happened. I can only imagine.

He sat listening to the steady beat of the rock' n' roll music. It calmed him down and slowed his thoughts. She'd been on his mind all day, every day. He'd walked to her grave yesterday and written a poem, not in her honor so much, but just as a way to express his pain.

He hadn't seen her body. She was cremated the day he flew home from England. His parents said she no longer looked like herself. They didn't want him to see the puffed up, bruised monster she had become. He took his parents' word that she was dead, but sometimes in the wee early morning hours he wondered if it were all a cruel hoax. He liked to imagine that she was really still alive and that she would suddenly appear and wonder at the crazed half-lives of the people she'd left behind.

He would be going back to England soon, and needing something tangible of hers, had gone into her room and selected one of her CDs to play back in his bedroom. As he listened to the music she loved, he felt, once again, their closeness. This was the shared experience he had missed having with her these past dreary six weeks.

As the music played, they were together again, laughing at each other's imitations, joking about Mom and Dad, playing tennis together, running in the autumn leaves to the quarry, playing with the dogs. He felt her hug as she told him goodbye the last time he'd seen her. She'd kissed him, in a playful manner, European style, on both of his cheeks. In his mind, he saw her smile and admired her quiet competence. He heard her speaking French to him and replied, en francaise.

Through the music she lifted him up, drew him to her. And then his mother's voice cut through him, wrenching him back to reality:

"Is that Elizabeth's CD you're listening to? Please put it back in her room. I want to keep it there on the shelf with the others. Her CDs might become mixed up with yours."

He put the CD on his sister's shelf and walked out of the room, a link to her denied. Maybe her music couldn't be mixed with his, but her life would always be part of him. He had shelved the CD, but he could never shelve her.

"I guess as usual I didn't really follow the directions" Peggy said, "I wrote about the siblings, not from their vantage points." I reassured her that it didn't matter: whatever we wrote was okay.

Peggy:

In some ways, I wish they could write this and tell me their points of view, but then I am not sure I could stand to know the suffering they have endured.

I recoiled as Mike began making phone calls at 3 a.m. If he could just put off making those calls, it would all remain a dream. But once the calls were made, I knew my other kids would die a little bit too.

Julie received the phone call in Argentina, so far away. She should have been the one we were worried about, in a foreign country, on her own, at twenty-three. She was the one who topped my prayer list, the farthest out of my control. And yet with that phone call, she became totally responsible for herself, her parents no longer functioning to take care of her departure plans. No aid, no advice, just "GET HOME."

What were her thoughts on that long plane ride?

Sarah, awakened in the middle of the night: "GET HOME!" How did she drive through the night from her college ninety minutes away? Through tears, surely, and all alone. Arriving at the house she'd left just two days ago and going past Rebecca's empty room—with bed unmade, clothing on the floor—to her own room in its familiar physical state, but radiating the impending doom, the knowledge that life had forever changed.

John. It is John I've worried about most. Though all the kids have endured this loss, I am sorry he had to be part of finding Rebecca dead; he gave her CPR that didn't work. To see his strong dad sobbing and me lying on the kitchen floor after the paramedics arrived. Did he know she was dead then? Many kids his age have never even attended a funeral, yet at sixteen, he had to experience death as it was happening. I remember that, as we left the hospital ER, he offered to drive home. He must have been quick to see his parents' strength evaporating. But Mike said, "It's OK. I will drive."

As we all walked out, a nurse called for John. She handed him a blue velvet pouch holding the jewelry Rebecca had been wearing. I remember thinking they shouldn't have made John take it. At that moment, I still wanted to be the mom, taking care of someone, but I had already begun crumbling into my new role of bereaved mother.

Dottye wrote from her son Glenn's point of view. Glenn is a stand-up comedian:

"Heyyyyyyy!!!!! How's everybody doing? We've got some great entertainment tonight . . . "

So here I go again, standing in front of this crowd of people who are "daring" me to make them laugh. And I can do it! It's how I choose to live my life. It's why I was born. And it is easy to go from town to town, crowd to crowd. Keep on moving. Make some noise. Let them think I'm always this happy, this funny, just flyin' high!

It's a good thing, isn't it? Helping folks have fun. Makin' 'em laugh or at least smile or raise an eyebrow. That's what I love, seeing life right before my eyes. Faces full of expectation. People lookin' for joy, happiness, a tickle to their funny bone.

Yes, I'm choosing this as my life's work because if I turn around and look behind me, I see the ghosts and I feel my feet slide away and I know my big brother's gone.

NAH. Not going there. Laughing is good. Making other people laugh is even better.

And on those rare nights when the crowd is quiet or distracted, somber or just not in the mood for my jokes? Or me? Hey, doesn't bother me. Rejection by strangers can't touch me. I've been to a way worse place. My big brother's gone.

"Hey! Did you hear the one about . . ."

Bereaved mothers are so busy ministering to members of their own families, not to mention all the other people they prop up—at the grocery store, at work, all those folks who cry and feel so bad and "don't know what to say" —that they often have trouble finding time for their own grief. So, as you might have noticed, I make sure to plan plenty of prompts around self-care.

We made and shared lists of *ways we give to ourselves,* or try to. Hearing each other's gave us all good ideas for ourselves.

Kathy:
· *Taking trips with my mom.*
· *Working out with weights, now that I can. I trembled for months after the accident and couldn't.*
· *Working on the boys' memorial perennial garden.*

Kay:
· *Yoga class on Saturday mornings for an hour and a half before taking care of Mother the rest of the day.*
· *Breathing!*
· *Being in the moment.*
· *Planning my garden. It's good to watch things come back year after year and to feed the birds out back.*
· *A talk with the upholstery man, whose son died the same day as Elizabeth.*

Dottye:
- *"Grandma fixes," time with my grandchildren.*
- *Cleaning the glass and debris out of our creek so we can play in it, the way I played as a child.*
- *Vegging in front of the den fire—watching it burn.*
- *Coffee with Mama every morning.*
- *I'm more conscious of my tendency to be Master of the Universe.*
- *My weight needs attention: I eat like a cow and I look like a cow and I don't care. But it doesn't feel good.*

Julie:
- *I want to spend time with friends but it's hard because I can't really make friends with the people in Dan's church. You know, the minister's wife. And we've moved so often.*
- *I like yoga and spending time in my favorite chair.*

Betsy:
- *Writing historical fiction about my home, Weston.*
- *I bought a swivel chair that feels so good to sit in after writing for two or three hours.*
- *Tending the colorful bed of impatiens plants.*

Peggy:
- *Doing art.*
- *Writing about and drawing the stuff in my house.*
- *Having a cleaning lady—that's a wonderful new thing.*

Beth:
- *Tutoring dyslexic children two afternoons a week.*
- *Exercising.*
- *My husband and I are doing a community project together, a five-year commitment to raise money for a hospitality house, like a Ronald McDonald house, for adults.*
- *Working with the community to do a Hospice addition. Planning the art for three buildings.*

We talked about a study at the Harvard Business School showing that MBAs who wrote down their goals were much more likely, ten years out, to meet those goals and be successful than students who didn't. Something magical happens when we write things down. By writing down our self-care goals we're more likely to pay attention to them.

On breaks, some of us hiked the trails that meander magically around a golf course and lake. Others napped, read, or sat out on the back patio enjoying the view. We moved from the living room into the sunroom, also off the patio. Couches lined two walls and a square game table sat in the middle of this room. This house had been in Beth's family all her life—the one next door belonged to her husband's family. They must have played here together as children, as did their own three children. I imagined the hours of cards and jigsaw puzzles this room had witnessed.

In the sun-warmed room was where we wrote in response to the essay by Brian Coyle, "Joyas Voladoras," about hearts.

Kathy:

A mother's heart is infinite; no matter how full, how sad, how hopeless, there is room in a mother's heart for her child's needs. "Your son is dead"…my heart collapses. "Your friends' children are both dead"…my heart screams.

I walk around the curtain in the emergency room and my son says "Hey Mama," and my heart leaps for joy. Who knew that the heart could hold such diverse emotions at the same time and not explode? There are no manuals to tell you how to cope, but your heart leads the way. It is a mystery, but if you can quiet your body and mind, your heart will always point you in the right direction.

It is almost unbelievable that the human heart can beat continuously hour after hour, day after day, year after year for 80, 90 or 100 years. Equally amazing is the heart's capacity to hold emotion. On the day a woman becomes a mother her heart expands to many times its original size, much like the Grinch, whose heart grew three sizes in one day.

Heart is so much more than the physical; it is mystical, emotional, spiritual. The best gift any child can receive is the true, complete, and pure love of a mother's heart.

I had asked each woman to bring a photo from her own childhood. We wrote about those—and read, sorry everyone wasn't there to learn more about each other's earlier lives. A photo from childhood offers a break from some of our more urgent prompts and lets us reconsider the past with fresh perspective.

That weekend we also wrote about ghosts and about gifts—those we had and used, those we didn't use but wanted to, and those we would start using.

Kathy volunteered to host a day-long session at her house in Winston-Salem in the spring. Those of us from out of town would come in the Friday night before. We'd all gather for dinner and the locals in the group (eight of the thirteen lived in and around "Winston") would put up the out-of-towners. We'd finish Saturday afternoon. Kay told us that her yoga teacher wanted to offer our group a class. We'd meet at Kathy's in the morning for breakfast and to write, go off to yoga together if that worked out, then head back to Kathy's for lunch and more writing.

It wouldn't be an entire weekend away, but it was better than nothing. In the meantime, we would find other ways to stay connected.

YOGA

I wanted to sample a yoga class with Kay's teacher, Sydney Hughes-McGee (pictured above), before taking the whole group—it's always a good idea to try something out ahead of time if you can. Since Winston-Salem was only about eighty miles from my home in Chapel Hill, I could easily drive over for part of a day. Kay and Monica joined me for a morning class.

"Don't look at me during the hour," Monica warned as we hung our jackets in the changing room and took off our shoes. "I'll laugh and maybe pass wind."

I had told her about going with my mother to yoga in a local church basement when I was a teenager—my presence dramatically lowered the median age. My mother's teacher was an eccentric local woman who would say things like, "Let the air move through and around you." The middle-aged women breathed heavily, groaned, and, sometimes "passed wind." And I would have to bite my towel (we didn't have mats back then) to try to squelch my laughter. Sometimes I couldn't contain the honking and snorts that escaped out my nose.

"Don't worry," I said to Monica. "I won't look at you. I'm going to try to ignore you!"

During Sydney's class, no one moaned or loudly passed air, but they could have and Sydney wouldn't have minded. Some people have a way of making everybody feel okay about their bodies, no matter how odd or misshapen. Sydney has that gift. Tall and regal herself, she had a gentle calm voice and she offered variations on all the poses, for different body types. "You don't ever want to feel tight or uneasy," she said, smiling.

How is it that some teachers seem so wide-open you can walk up to them after class, show them the hump in your back or the crooked toes you've been hiding all your life, and say, "Look at this. Got any suggestions?" And feel fine doing it.

We set a date to bring the group.

Monica, Kay, and I came out of the building into the late morning sun, feeling relaxed and stretched, eager to head to their favorite café for coffee. As we approached the parking area, Monica laughed and pointed. "Looks like somebody really liked your car." My roof and front hood were covered with white bird droppings. Kay's and Monica's cars, on either side of mine, were pristine, completely unsoiled.

"Well," Monica added, with an impish shrug and sideways glance. "I think your mother's yoga teacher sent the birds. Payback for laughing in her class. Sorry."

Later that week, I got a small package in the mail—inside was a white mug featuring a black and white cartoon: two birds sit on a wire watching a man scrub his car, a hose beside him, beads of sweat on his brow.

One bird says to the other: "Wait till he's finished."

A few days later, an email arrived from Kelly:
Okay, everybody. I'm pregnant. And it's a GIRL! We found out this morning. The boys are excited and David is going out to buy the pink paint.

I will miss you all next weekend and will miss the yoga. My body could use some relaxation.

Kelly was ecstatic to be having another girl. We were about to have two baby girls join our group, Kelly's and Hope, from China.

A few years later, Kelly wrote:

Katie Gray—She always smells faintly of candy. It might be because she hides in the pantry and eats it! The smell reminds me of stirring a large, bubbling copper vat—preparing to make caramel apples in the fall. Even when she has wallowed in the sand box and run in the park for hours, she still smells sugary and light. For some reason, I have lost the smell of Abby—maybe I can vaguely remember her milky breath, but when I try to associate the smell with her, the face blurs and morphs into Cameron or Cohen or Katie Gray.

We met on a Saturday in Kathy's sunken den, a plush room with stained wood paneling and grass cloth wallpaper. Everyone admired the portraits of Wesley and Ryan, ages four and two and smaller portraits of all three children. Some of us sat on furniture and others lounged on the carpeted floor.

After a warm-up prompt, I asked Monica to read a poem by Denise Levertov called "Talking to Grief." Monica's fear of public speaking sometimes made her reluctant to read her own work. Having her read aloud something by somebody else might help her.

"You know," she had told me earlier, "there are people who fear public speaking more than death. I'm one of them."

Voice quivering, Monica got through the poem.

We wrote about grief, what it looks like, feels like, where it lives. Dottye read about how grief is a big old bathtub and that she needs to get in it, wallow in it, sit in there, and not run away. Kathy wrote about the shame of guilt, how it closes you up in a closet and won't let you out. Beth wrote about cancer and all the people she knows who were suffering and dying from the disease. Julie worked with an image of a crater and falling down into it and the need to find a way to spiral up and out.

On a break, we got a tour of Kathy's house, including Ryan's room, where the family still maintained his fish tank.

127

We then piled into two cars and headed to the yoga studio.

Sydney had placed purple and blue yoga mats in a sun pattern so that they looked like rays. "Breath of sol," somebody said. She had us lie down so that that our feet pointed towards the middle of the space. She had placed fresh pink and red rose petals on the floor around the mats, like fragrant confetti.

We each lay down on a mat and settled into the quiet. We had never done anything like this together before—gone out as a group to take a class. Sydney used easy poses, encouraging us to twist our spines and let our hips relax. She focused on expanding the space around our hearts and deepening our breathing. At the end of the hour she read to us from a text about restoring our spirits. I dozed in the final restful pose, flat on my back.

I didn't find out until we got back to Kathy's that Peggy had almost had a meltdown in the yoga class. She was riding in the other car and sobbed to everybody in that group about the physical and mental anguish she'd felt during class. She needed to be drawing, moving around, or writing. She'd been in agony, and none of us had even known.

Feeling contrite, I realized I should have been keeping an eye on everybody. I was still the group leader and responsible for everyone, even though somebody else was taking us through an experience.

"I wish you had just gotten up and left the room," I said. "Sydney would have understood."

"I felt too self-conscious and like I was a bad girl for not getting into the yoga with everybody."

"You just can't go anywhere without your art materials," I said, "and you always have permission to draw—wherever we are. From now on you don't have to do anything we all do together, except write, of course."

I suggested we write about how our bodies felt after the yoga class and what stayed with us from the experience. "Peggy, you can draw how you felt but do write about it too. It might be helpful for you."

"You mean I have to think MORE about yoga?"

"Yup," I said. "You do."

"Nobody said this group was going to be fun," Monica said, with her little shrug. "It's like Catholic school. Right, Peggy?"

I read a Margaret Atwood poem, "The Country Beneath the Earth," about those who live in the underworld and what they have to teach us, providing we can "descend and return safely." We talked about the Demeter- Persephone myth. And how Persephone wasn't able to return permanently from the underworld because she had eaten the pomegranate seeds—once someone eats in the underworld she can never leave it forever.

When Persephone comes above ground, her mother Demeter, goddess of the harvest, celebrates with spring blossoms and trees in bloom and the harvest in the fall. But when Persephone goes back to Hades and the underworld, Demeter grieves and all the leaves fall from the trees, the ground hardens, and we have winter. All of us could identify with the notion that grief is cyclical. It never disappears; rather, it has phases. Once we've been in the underworld we can never again live above ground all the time.

We wrote about the underworld.

Someone had sent me an article about forgiveness from a journal on women's health. There were bullets about how forgiveness can bring healing. "How do you all feel about forgiveness?" I asked. "Let's write about that."

"This is extremely difficult for me," Kathy said. "I just don't think I can write about forgiveness now."

"Then don't," I said. "Remember: you don't ever have to respond to a prompt. You can write about anything you want or not write at all—though I will always encourage you to write, since we give ourselves so little time for writing and the reflection and insight that comes with it."

"But you made me write about yoga," Peggy said.

"Yes, but you know you didn't *have* to."

After the weekend, Sydney admitted to me that she had been terrified at the thought of teaching us, a group of bereaved moms. "I have a four-year-old son and even the thought of what you'd all been through" she said, "I just couldn't bear it." But once she had met us and seen how goofy and human we were, she relaxed.

Kay:

I wanted to share an email (with Sydney's permission) that she sent this morning about our session with her at Arts of Yoga yesterday.

With our hearts on my mind,

Kay

Dear Kay,

Giving that class to your group was one of the most meaningful things I have ever done. I can't stop thinking about it and thinking about each of you. My husband's father died in a truck accident when Tony was a teenager. And then his grandmother died about ten years later from lung cancer. It just occurred to me yesterday, witnessing the love and support in your group, how wonderful it could have been for her if she'd had a group like yours. I know that in Chinese medicine the lungs are associated with grief, and I've wondered if she had enough support through her grief over her son. What you are doing together is so important and it calms my heart to know that such groups exist.

When Beverly said that she was adopting a child from China, I knew she was the mother of the two boys who died on First St. I remember being aware of that devastating accident. This morning I looked for more information about Kwan Yin (the statue in the studio). I knew that she had a special relationship to mothers and children, but really didn't know more. Reading about her this morning it occurs to me that Beverly should have a Kwan Yin statue! She is the feminine face of God in Asia, the Compassionate Mother.

Perhaps you are familiar with her. The story goes that she was about to walk through the gates of heaven when she heard the cries of the world, and chose to turn back to be here for those who are suffering. She has a special relationship with mothers and children and is whom a woman calls on when she longs for a child. Apparently her statues can be found in temples all over China and are often placed in little outside altars, usually beside streams, lakes, and the ocean. People visit her daily and bring their struggles and she responds always with compassion and understanding. Perhaps little Hope would enjoy her, and maybe she would bring some peace to Beverly as she mothers Hope.

Email from Beverly:

Hello dear friends,

I stood here at my kitchen desk reading Sydney's email and had shivers and blurred vision from her thoughtful remarks. Quite serendipitous! I will certainly look for Kwan Yin in China for my garden and put it in a special spot for our new family to enjoy. . .

EMERALD ISLE

Everyone was particularly psyched for our next weekend retreat. We were going to the beach together for a weekend on the North Carolina coast. Scharme had a modest four-bedroom house on the sound at Emerald Isle. Her friend across the street, who volunteered his house, had four more bedrooms.

For me, the beach trumps just about every other place on earth. I love to walk barefoot and listen to the beat of surf; watch the ripply sand patterns, the color shifts in the water, the swells rising up like giant commas before curling and crashing. My mother always said that gazing at a distant water horizon is medicine for the eye muscles and, I would add, the spirit. She also said that walking in knee-high water helps the circulation and that walking in sand gave the best pedicure. Some people prefer mountain scapes. I love the piney breezes, but mountains remind me of movie backdrops; they seem immutable, static, silent. This has its appeal, but the ocean never stops calling and glistening and flirting. And I live to body surf.

Kay:

On Beaches

I am about to travel to a beach for the fourth time in as many weeks. The occasions for the three other trips—to have a reunion with cousins and to help my son and his family pack their belongings and move from a northern Outer Banks beach to a southern North Carolina beach—are different from the beach trip I'm now preparing for. I'm going to Emerald Isle to meet the twelve mothers who have been a source of solace, healing and friendship.

And in the movies in my mind as I get ready for this trip—in a strange way, it's a vacation for my lost daughter and me—I keep seeing frozen frames from past trips. Play—Pause—Rewind—Play. I see my daughter Elizabeth as a toddler in an orange and yellow striped Sesame Street swim suit standing in front of a patch of orange and yellow gaillardia and scrubby sea grasses. Her tight blonde curls encircle her face and her blue eyes gaze directly at the camera. I see another frame with Elizabeth as an eight-year-old—lanky and long-legged and leaping on the open white expanse of Ocracoke Island beach, her blonde hair flying and frizzing about her face. More frames float by, but these two persist.

Beaches and seas bring me back to my need for quiet, for introspection, for observation, for the iambic rhythm of the waves. On the first Saturday morning that our group of bereaved mothers met for writing, I wrote to a prompt about a healing place, a safe place. I'm returning to that place now as I prepare to meet my "sisters" at the beach.

There was certainly something else special about this weekend.

"Would it be okay to bring Katie Gray," Kelly had asked me, "since I'm still breast-feeding?"

The decision was unanimous. "Of course," we all said.

I compared this robust enthusiasm to the women's coolness when Kelly had brought baby Cohen that bleak March morning of our second session.

"I promise," Kelly said. "This is my last baby. I won't be bringing any more to the group."

Kelly was driving from her house in the mountains to pick up Beverly; they would ride together to the beach so that Beverly could experience being with a baby again—and a girl this time. "I need all the practice I can get," Beverly said, "being so old and all."

Beverly and her husband Blaine had been caught up in the Byzantine paperwork and bureaucracy of adopting their girl from China. One setback involved Beverly's fingerprints having to be redone.

"I seem to have rubbed my prints bare," she said, after the first set came back without lines. "I have no identity. Too much scrubbing."

Each delay meant a longer wait. Every month a group of approved parents received notification that they would be leaving within a few weeks for China, and every month Beverly and Blaine were not on the list. She sent periodic email updates.

"I just have to trust that my little girl is out there," Beverly wrote, "and that we'll get to her, eventually."

When Kelly and Katie Gray and Beverly walked in, every set of arms reached out to that baby. "Our mascot," somebody said. "We'll take turns holding her all weekend."

"We don't need our little red beanie baby bear anymore," Monica added. "We can pass around Katie Gray."

That first afternoon, we took a long time settling down. I decided to offer a different opening prompt, to capitalize on the good humor and energy within the group. Instead of writing about what matters or what's going on, I told everyone to write a brief autobiographical piece—in five minutes—and to include one lie in it.

Pat Schneider sometimes uses this prompt as an icebreaker at the beginning of a residency. It's a hands-on way to experience the difference between fiction and nonfiction. And it encourages good listening and practice paying close attention—trying to detect the lie! And of course it's a way to get to know each other better. We knew a lot about each other's present lives in this group. Here was a way, like writing about our childhood photos, to lean again into each other's pasts.

As we wrote, instead of our customary silence, we heard Katie Gray's delightful gurgling and sucking at her mother's breast.

Some women make motherhood look so luscious. Kelly is one of them. She breastfed and wrote at the same time, her journal angled beside her, Katie sprawled over her chest. At the end of the writing session, while Katie Gray's perfect little heart-shaped mouth opened wider and then closed slightly as she slept in Kelly's lap, we had a little contest. Someone would read and then the group got only three chances to guess the lie.

Kay's narratives included these truths:

—*I was a cheerleader who didn't know the rules of football and cheered at the wrong time.*

—*I had a photo made with Mohammed Ali in Chicago when one of my students asked him to cheer me up.*

—*My daughter wrote a letter to Queen Elizabeth inviting her to tea in Tobaccoville and asking if she really sat on a windowsill in Roald Dahl's book, BFG.*

And this lie that Julie guessed ("I have a good built-in lie detector," she told us, "from being a minister."):

—*Through extensive genealogical research, I have learned that I am a distant relative of Queen Elizabeth II. Even though her name is Elizabeth Windsor Mountbatten, we are related through Smiths, Joneses and Linvilles.*

Somebody wrote about sleeping with a priest; somebody else about getting a "D" in oceanography, another about having sex in an elevator. We laughed and tried to coax out each other's lies. Mine was simple and benign—that my long braids lifted as I pumped in a swing. Kay guessed it. "When you were that young you didn't have braids and long hair."

I thought how far we had come from our first meeting in that cold college board room. And now here we were on the coast on a sparkly day, passing around a healthy baby and making up stories.

Anne Morrow Lindbergh is a favorite author of ours, in part because she too lost a child. I had read to the group from her memoir, *Hours of Lead, Hours of Gold,* about her son's kidnapping and death. On this shimmery end-of-summer day at the beach, our leaden collective grief seemed to be morphing into gold or at least bronze. I asked everyone to take a walk on the beach and to do what Lindbergh suggests in *Gift From the Sea.*

"Let a shell or an object find you," I said. "Bring them back and we'll write about them later."

135

"Homework?" Monica asked, "at the beach?" She scrunched up her face.

"Careful," I said, "or you'll have to stay after class and write one hundred times: 'I will not act up anymore.'"

It was glorious walking weather and I now understood how Emerald Isle got its name. The water is in fact emerald green. Some of us took turns holding Katie Gray above the rushing surf line; others traipsed off alone or in small groups to walk the beach. Julie usually chose a solitary walk. She was the mother of two young children and clearly needed solitude while others, like Scharme who lives alone, children grown, could often be found in the company of others.

We ate fresh boiled shrimp out on Scharme's back deck. Her yard was bordered by pink-blooming oleanders and bushes laced with writing spiders, given that name because they weave what looks like letters into their webs. An incandescent sunset reflected off the Intracoastal Waterway, turning the world shades of orange and red and peach.

After dinner Scharme brought out a 1950s children's book about seashells, so that we could look up the shells we had gathered on our walks. We laughed about the big-lipped drill snail, our "Julia Roberts by the sea." We tried to imagine what sort of creature had lived in some of our found shells and the type we'd choose to inhabit, if we had to.

Several women stayed up late that night, playing Scrabble. Somebody commented that all new babies look like Winston Churchill but Beverly said, "My Chinese baby is not going to look like Winston Churchill."

Not much for board games, I went to my bedroom early, a simple breezy room looking out on the water. Scharme had insisted I have my own space, which I appreciated—and since then have always tried to negotiate—and I lay in bed, the sound of laughter wafting in from the living room.

It was delightful to overhear how easily the group members interacted. A friend had asked me if there were cliques in the group and I said no. I think we all experience the group deeply and honor each other. We don't judge each other; we don't gossip about each other; we don't compare our losses. That same friend asked me if the group divided between those who lost young children and those who lost adults. No, I told her. We all understood loss and that was what mattered. My friend told me about a woman she knew who only wanted to find women with stories close to her own—her eight-year-old son died of leukemia. She couldn't relate to women who had lost babies or grown children. Our group isn't that way: the writing helps. On the page we share our experiences of loss and of so many other parts of our lives too. We're able to respect our differences and appreciate our commonality.

Over breakfast, we heard about the night's drama. Monica and Peggy were the last to turn in; they were staying across the road at Howard's house. (The women now write him fan mail thank you letters every time we stay there.)

"So we get back to Howard's—after Peggy fell in a hole crossing the neighbor's yard," Monica said, "and we start up the stairs to the house."

"There was a real hole in the yard," Peggy added. "I saw it this morning. I wasn't drunk or anything, I just fell in a hole."

"Yeah, sure," Beverly said.

To enter, they had to climb an outside staircase. "Fortunately we'd had our wits about us and left a light on," Peggy said.

Monica gave her a short stare. "What? The wimps who turned in early left the light on—Kay and that crowd."

"Well, anyway, at the top of the stairs, blocking the door, was a possum," Peggy said. "We were going to come get you up, Carol, but then Monica had an idea."

"Thank god," I said. "Everybody knows Monica is the problem solver, not me."

"Thank you," Monica said. "I haven't been a nurse, giving enemas all these years, for nothing. I found a hose in the driveway, turned it on hard, and gave that possum a shot in the rear he'll never forget."

The possum skittered down the stairs and disappeared into the dark night.

Somebody looked up "possum" in Scharme's encyclopedia and learned they are the only marsupials in North America.

"Hey, no offense to Katie Gray but maybe the possum ought to be our mascot," I volunteered. "They hold their children in a pouch close to their hearts, just like we do."

"And they'll eat just about anything," Monica said. "Just like us."

"You know what?" Beverly said, "I bet I've got a recipe for possum. Growing up in the country, we really did eat anything."

After researching possums, we talked about how much fun it is to make up "pseudo-scientific" information. Ever since, whenever we can, we've enjoyed applying our pseudo-science, in the form of half-baked theories, to seashells, spiders, rock outcroppings, weather, sunsets, the history of mountains, and fog.

Whenever anybody wanted to hold Katie Gray, Kelly would break into her deep-dimpled pretty smile and hand her baby over. She was trusting, relaxed—even though we all knew Katie wore a monitor at night and Kelly vigilantly watched to make sure her little chest moved up and down. Sometimes Kelly fell asleep writing and so did Katie Gray, sprawled across her lap, both of them with their perfect mouths barely open.

Some of us explored the ocean every day—Barbara, Beverly, and I. Barbara swam way out alone, then up and down the coast. I body surfed, Beverly hopped up and down and pushed herself up over waves—keeping her hair dry. I thought about how our athletic selves show a lot about us. Barbara is a loner; I crave the pounding waves pummeling my muscles; Beverly loves the water but likes to be a buoy, a beacon above the surface.

Dottye took a long bike ride down the beach road, "It was easy on the way," she said. "I just glided and rode, my worries blowing away. I had forgotten how easy bike riding was. I didn't realize the breeze was behind me. I barely made it back, had to walk the bike, going into the wind."

We took turns caring for and changing Katie Gray. She didn't cry once all weekend. Her baby carrier was our centerpiece, our shrine.

On Sunday, Scharme invited us back for the next year, same time, same place. We made plans to meet in the spring and came up with a group list of things to focus on before next time.

To-Go Prompts:
1. Do something risque/fun
2. Simplify
3. Be more reflective and WRITE more
4. Explore some pseudo-science

Before we left, Scharme made a list. This Weekend:

Three Night Pajama Party
Peeling shrimp
 Chocolate cake
Personal tales—true and false
Late night chats
Walks on the beach, sand in our shoes
Shells calling our names
Simplifying lives
Butterflies—dancing just for us
Our children's spirits ever by our sides
Brighter smiles, lighter hearts
Bountiful "comfort food"
Needles knitting
Sudoku slipped from beneath the sofa when Carol wasn't looking
(shame on you Monica)
Walking Katie Gray
Missing my dog Blueberry
Sheer awe at our Sisters' words, springing off the pages directly into our
hearts
 Sharing the lives of the children we so dearly miss.
A circle of friends doing together what we cannot do alone.

Betsy wasn't able to join us but we sent her prompts and updates.
She wrote to us:
Here is a poem I wrote about the beach weekend I missed. Carol is made
out to be a drillmaster, which, as you all know, she is not. You all said something
about a drill (that's a type of shell) on the beach, which struck me as funny: a
drill with rasping lips!

The Drill and Drillers

The drill sat with rasping lips
Upon the wetted sandwiched sand.
His fleshy meal
A fine repast.
But ho! What drill is he
Compared to mighty drill
 Master she?

The Master sits with pen in hand
Tap tapping the Sols to order.
You must write and write and
Write your best so many a soul
Can see,
How life is cruel and sometimes harsh
But Hope eternal springs.
Now rise up and swim,
Conquer those waves.
Battle the creeping bulge.
Arm yourselves with words of
Passion and live your
Lives of strength
And courage.

One missed the drill but
Wrote, in keeping with her sisters.
Her absence sore felt but
Not as keenly as
Those fourteen who
Gathered 'round
With loving thoughts
To watch
The driller's drill,
With rasping lips
And joyful hearts.

Soon after the weekend, Kelly emailed us. Here's part of the list she sent.

Katie Gray is scheduled for her first shots on Monday:
- *Could not seem to take seriously, expect myself to go to the appointment.*
- *I dread the idea of introducing her body to these vaccinations.*
- *Would Abby be alive today if she hadn't had those shots?*
- *Called David two times on his cell phone at 7:30 and 7:35. What do I do?*
- *Just go or don't go was his reply.*
- *I'm not a blind follower of DOCTORS anymore.*
- *I prayed for guidance but none came.*
- *Maybe I just was not listening closely enough.*
- *Called at 7:42 to reschedule...for next Tuesday 8:00 am.*
- *Will keep you posted.*

RESEARCH TRIP

Between meetings I visited Winston-Salem to spend time with several of the women and to look at photos, bedrooms, accident sites, and graves.

Dottye and I met in the lobby of the hospital where she worked. We had planned to drive to the park where Alex shot himself. "You know," she said, "I just don't feel up to it today. Let's get something to eat here."

She told me over soup and sandwiches that every January, around the time of Alex's suicide, she goes into a depression. "It's in my body, this season," she said. "I can't do anything except endure it."

Later that day Kay and I drove to the Moravian church cemetery, called God's Acre, where her daughter Elizabeth is buried. We sat in the parked car for a while, talking. Kay pointed at the church doors and remembered that she had trouble staying beside the coffin

when the pallbearers wheeled it out of the church and delivered it to the graveyard. "I had to run along to keep up," Kay said, placing her right hand over her heart as she spoke—that gesture again that she picked up after her daughter's death.

"Elizabeth was always rushing ahead—to the wonderful new thing," Kay said. "Even, it turned out, her own burial." Her velvety voice was softer than usual. The money used to buy that coffin on wheels could have purchased a car for Elizabeth, had she lived to be sixteen.

As Kay spoke, I pondered the impossible: saying a front-door goodbye to your daughter on a brisk Friday autumn afternoon, expecting to see her sunny, lanky frame cross back over the home threshold in a few hours, but instead saying a final goodbye to her, three days later, in her coffin.

We got out of the car. A sharp wind rushed across the open space and right through my thin wool sweater. We walked under a wrought iron arch and approached the cemetery, a vast grassy expanse of symmetrical white stones laid out like tiles, against a backdrop of hardwoods at the far edges.

"All the graves face East," Kay said, "So they can greet the new day. The gravestones are all the same because Moravians believe that in death we're all equal. We call it democracy in death."

I thought of a line a workshop student wrote to the prompt "Write your own obituary." She quoted her father who had often said. "Shrouds have no pockets."

Here, no one merits a more elaborate memorial structure than anyone else. There are no fancy angels or crypts or shiny black marble tombstones. People are buried in the order in which they die; Elizabeth's grave is next to a woman who died in her eighties, just before Elizabeth died. The two had never met.

The damp grass squished under our feet as we walked toward the back of the acre and Elizabeth's grave. The only distinguishing feature of these stones is that the children's squares are smaller. Not Elizabeth's. At fifteen, she was no longer considered a child.

The Moravian Church meant a lot to Elizabeth, Kay said. She had enjoyed the church youth group and responded deeply to one of the church credos:

In essentials unity. In non-essentials liberty. In all things love. "Those words summed up Elizabeth's basic beliefs," Kay told me.

We arrived at Elizabeth's gravestone. It was a lovely spot. The rows and rows of matching flat stones in this silent place felt somehow comforting, safe. Kay told me that sometimes she comes to this place to write.

Kay and I stood quietly for some time before heading back to the car. The sun was dipping low in the sky and the wind continued to blow hard. I thought of the picture Kay shared of Elizabeth, dancing wildly in bare feet and a flowery long dress, her disheveled blonde hair blowing around her face, like this wind in the tree branches. The weather seemed fitting—crisp, clear, chilly, alive with breeze. The air and clouds moved fast, like Elizabeth.

I told Kay that, ever since we scattered Malcolm's ashes in the ocean, I have always felt at home and close to my son when I'm near an ocean. It doesn't matter which one.

That evening Scharme and I sat down in her leaded-glass windowed dining room to a delicious home-cooked meal. "I feel awkward in the group sometimes," Scharme said, "Steve's life was so complicated and the details of his death so sordid and disturbing, that I don't want to share much about him."

"I can understand feeling that way," I said," but you know you can write anything with this group."

"I know," she said, "and I will write more about him in time, and read those pieces to the group. Just not yet."

She gave me some background information. Steve had been diagnosed with multiple personalities; he had claimed to have lovers and illnesses he didn't have. "He was a very disturbed man," she said.

We looked at pictures of Steve and she told me about his death. "He was living in a trailer in Tennessee and spent time with a bad group of people. I wouldn't call them friends." She read me some of her more private pieces.

Suicide
When will that door open?
"Hi, Mom, I'm here, I'm home."
What did they do to you?

Why wouldn't they listen to me?

What were you thinking? What was so bad you couldn't call me for help?

Surely that was a mistake. That wasn't you on that steel table—it did not even look like you—cold, unkempt, still, grey. That wasn't my Steve; surely to God this is somebody else, not you, not Steve.

What did I do?

What didn't I do?

Our last phone conversation—tenuous at best.

Your last message—angry.

My letters—unanswered. Did you even get them?

"Tough love," they told me. Why did I listen?

"Follow your heart," I say—damned if I do, damned if I don't.

Where did I go wrong?

I drove you away; I know I did.

That was my fault.

My head knows you were ill, not yourself—you were many men, but none was Steve. The Steve I know didn't like the people he had become. He couldn't live with them any longer. They were not him; they were nothing like the real Steve. They were hurting everyone he touched, all those he loved; he could not stop them. Friends deserted him when he needed them most. Some retreated, not knowing how to help. I held on, waiting for the call that never came. Then it was too late.

Scharme had also written from Steve's point of view:

Suicide: the mental disease

Trapper. . . You have cornered me.

Thief . . . You stole my head. You stole my heart. They once met. Then they did not.

Destroyer . . . You smashed my dreams, crushed my hopes, shattered my strength.

Murderer . . . You killed my soul, all that was good in me. You left me a being I do not know.

Deserter . . . You left me with no way out.

I am so sorry. I am tired of struggling. It is time for me to go home.

145

"Thank you for reading me those pieces," I said. "I know how hard that was for you."

I took another bite of chicken and rice and sipped my wine. Scharme was razor thin. I never saw her eat much. She always served wine to others, though she never drank anything herself but coffee and Tab. Now she sat looking through her writings, not touching anything on her plate. A short piece:

This morning I am scheduled to talk at an AA meeting. I am a "wreck." It makes me so nervous even though it is just my story. In the eleven years before Steve's death, we enjoyed giving Mother-Son talks together. I wasn't as nervous then because I would share a little and then introduce Steve, who thrived on being in the limelight. He could hold a group in the palm of his hand—have them laughing and crying at the same time. Oh how I want him by my side today.

I decided to take a walk in the park, beforehand, as I do every day. In the four years Steve has been gone, I've struggled to hear his voice but it just would not come. On the other hand I feel his presence everywhere, especially in the park—a mallard bathing in the creek, the bird singing in the tree, the breeze, the sun; he is there.

But this morning when I needed to feel his nearness so badly, I did not. This really disturbed me. But I know he is always in my heart, so I headed home. When I got back, my newspaper was in the yard and I reached down to pick it up and right in the middle of the front page was a lovely dollop of bird poop. And I clearly heard his voice say "Gotcha Mom—I'm here," followed by his laughter which always came when he knew he had succeeded with one of his practical jokes. This was just what I needed—it was no coincidence.

Something about Scharme set her apart from the others in the group. She lived alone. That was part of it. All the other women are married, living with a man and often children. Scharme was divorced, amiably. Maybe it was also because she had invited me a few times to stay with her and work with her on her writing, one on one. We had spent long hours talking into the night, me wrapped up in a blanket and stretched out on the couch, Scharme sitting in her favorite upholstered chair.

"Would you like to go down to Barbara's place with me this evening?" I asked. I was getting together with Barbara, who lived nearby, to check out her house as a meeting venue. She had volunteered to host a weekend.

"No, you go alone. It's important for Barbara to show you around, and for you and Bud to get to know each other. I'll be up when you get back."

Barbara and Bud's large 1920s house had high-ceilinged, airy rooms and plenty of space for writing. Barbara led me back to the kitchen to meet Bud, who was sitting at their round table, sipping a glass of red wine.

We shook hands. Mine was damp—nerves. I wasn't sure about Bud, about our taking Barbara away from him for our meetings. I thought I was going to have to prove something when we finally met, but I wasn't sure what. Bud, however, was smiley and friendly, opening right up, asking me about myself, particularly my tennis game, and answering all my questions. I knew right away that he wasn't against the group. He was part of us, another grieving parent. He got it.

Barbara gave me a house tour, starting in the front hall. It was really more of a "William" tour. The house was a shrine to their boy. In the front, by the inner stairwell, photos lined the walls—of William, bald from chemo, standing (thanks to the Make-a-Wish Foundation) beside giant famous basketball players. There were pictures of William in sports uniforms, William with his parents. There was the poem Barbara and Bud wrote and read at his funeral, a verse for each of his eight years.

Upstairs in William's room, a trunk held all sorts of mementos: basketball cards, a basketball signed by some of the sports' greatest players, sweatshirts, William's wallet—still holding his money. In the living room, on the mantle sat an urn holding William's ashes.

"I don't know what to do with them, so they stay here," Barbara said. She told me about her brother who died traumatically, not long after William. "He and William were really close."

We settled in the kitchen and picked an April weekend for the meeting. We would have both Barbara's house and Scharme's, so there was plenty of room to put everybody up. And we hoped the other women who lived in town would choose to stay overnight too. It's special to wake up in the morning and sit around together in our pajamas over an early cup of coffee, before the writing begins.

The next day I met with Beverly. We drove down First Street to the accident site, past the "Adopt a Street" sign in memory of the three boys. We saw the replacement crepe myrtles a man had planted in his front yard and his reconstructed fence. The car had ripped through the man's fence and destroyed the shrubs. "The guy wrote and told me that he was replacing the pink crepe myrtles with three white-bloomers in memory of the three boys," Beverly said. She told me that the first person at the scene of the accident was a medical student who later reassured the Burtons and the Shoafs that all three boys had died instantly. He also sent Christmas cards to the families for several years, letting them know where he was and that he was thinking of them.

Beverly and I spent a few hours in a coffee shop while I pored over the memory books she had made in honor of her sons. At their memorial service, her husband's aunt had put out two stacks of Xeroxed sheets of paper for people to take. "What I remember about Andy" was on the top of one sheet and, on the other, "What I remember about Wes." She asked people to identify themselves and then answer a few questions: How did you know them? When did you know them? Memories you have of them. For months, years even, Beverly received these in the mail from people—story after story about her boys, things she didn't know.

"Some of their friends sent pages of memories," she told me. "Who ever knew teenaged boys could write so much?"

THE DEATH NARRATIVES

I had coffee recently with a young woman who lost her second child five years ago. She had sent me a short essay she wrote and was wondering about joining one of my writing groups for bereaved mothers. As we sat together on a café terrace overlooking a hardwood forest, she told me she was just then beginning to consider writing about the devastating details of her child's rather sudden death from a most unusual and undiagnosed (until too late) heart defect.

"I haven't felt I could face writing the whole story until now," she said, though it grips her insides all the time. I told her that our group met for four years before everybody wrote full narratives about their children's deaths—with a beginning, middle, and end.

This waiting was by design on my part. "Tell the whole truth but tell it slant," Emily Dickinson wrote. Many writers use that line. I interpret it to mean: tell it—the truth, the story—from an angle; look in through a crack in the door or a beam of light, and write about that sliver of room you see—the section of scarred dresser, a bit of cloudy mirror, the piece of neatly-made bed. Don't try to give a panorama of the entire house all at once.

Early on, give writers carefully selected prompts. Evoke a small piece of the mosaic, a patch of the quilt.

On the radio a while back, I heard a feature about a psychiatrist who had decided to use writing with severely depressed patients. At the first meeting, she told them to write about anything at all and they did, for twenty minutes. Encouraged, she said at the second meeting: "Write for twenty minutes. About anything." Again they wrote without guidance. On the third meeting, she told them to write once more. They refused—couldn't, wouldn't. Writing swamped and depressed them. It was too frightening, made them feel worse. Her open free writing sessions would have been like telling the bereaved mothers at our first meeting: "Write the whole story of your child's death."

Writing without moorings, can be dangerous—like setting out on a dark path without a flashlight or descending into a mine without a canary. With prompts we have starting points, new angles. The suggestions help to ease open, gently, the protective shells surrounding nuggets of thought or memory and get at the meat inside. A good prompt can let in light, bathe those stuck grimy areas, stir up a breeze. Prompts remind me of playground equipment. They free us to swing and climb, yet we always have something to hang onto—a chinning bar, a slide, a rope. They give us permission to probe; they also ground us. They are like the dock with the sturdy wooden ladder that we can always swim back to when we find ourselves in deep water, frightened and out of breath. Even if we choose not to use them, the suggestions will still often influence our writing.

The psychiatrist on the radio hadn't understood that we need guidance to venture into the unconscious, especially if we're vulnerable—and we're all vulnerable. We need a life jacket, which, incidentally, makes a great prompt. I often bring in two of those old "U" shaped orange ones with white cotton ties and neck rests.

Finally, at this meeting at Barbara's, I felt ready to offer the prompt I had held off giving for so long, to write the death narrative. Had we met weekly or monthly we might have approached the narratives sooner but we met only every six months.

I didn't open with the narratives that weekend, waiting until Saturday afternoon, when everybody was warmed up.

Scharme served dinner on Friday night, vegetarian and meat lasagnas, salad, and French bread. After dinner we cleared the large dark dining room table. I warned the women, to collective groans, that we were going to do an art project.

I gave each woman a piece of paper with a circle drawn on it, a blank mandala. I had put boxes of crayons and markers in the middle of the table.

"Using as many colors as you'd like, color the circle, letting your mind think over how you have felt since the death."

"I can't draw or do art, but here goes," Dottye said, picking up a crayon. "Look. Already, I've strayed outside the circle."

"It's all right," I said. "Anything goes."

The women giggled nervously but eventually focused on coloring—the only sounds were Katie Gray's gurglings and crayons rubbing on paper. After everybody finished, I asked each woman to tell us something about what she had drawn.

Every picture reflected the artist. Dottye's was sloppy, a dizzying set of circles enclosed a misshapen square. Barbara made tidy colorful triangles that looked like a stained glass window, the panes symmetrical and connected—one of them black. Many of the women's circles had black centers and black rings or tears within the mandala. Kathy wrote "Ryan" in the middle of her circle and drew wavy lines to connect it with the things she knew Ryan loved—the French horn, fish, dogs. There were musical notes and everywhere, clumps of tears. Beverly's included a heart in the center, bisected by a weeping cross. One side contained the word "Hope" in orange crayon, with a pink background. Julie's was the ocean; along the wave line she had printed the alphabet. Under the water were stars and a cluster of small ominous black circles. Her son Jack would have been learning to read, she explained. Mine was mostly cerulean blue, with a brown tree, and a yellow setting moon (though it looked more like a banana), all densely colored.

Before breaking and going to bed, some of us at Scharme's and others down the street at Barbara's, I invited the women to ask for a dream that night and to make sure they had pen and paper nearby. "Asking for dreams," I told them, "often works. Be prepared."

On Saturday morning, in Barbara's spacious living room, home to a pair of caged cockatiels, Barbara announced that Bud had something he wanted to show us. He entered and, without pause, peeled off his shirt, exposing a huge tattoo of William's face on his left shoulder.

"I wake up looking at that every morning," Barbara said, with a laugh.

After the shock wore off, we all admired the likeness to William, who we only knew from pictures and of course Barbara's writings.

"I like the background being my flesh," Bud said. "My flesh, William's image."

We wrote about "What's inside?" Beth read us a dream she had recorded from the night before: She and Sandy were going to a big show, something like the Academy Awards. They were coming from the beach, casually dressed. Beth carried with her a basket of clean but unfolded laundry and no purse. Everyone else at the event was in black tie. A woman with an x-ray machine was checking everybody's purses and said she'd keep the basket during the event. Beth regretted that the laundry wasn't folded.

It was odd, in the way dreams are, that Beth, always nicely dressed in ironed slacks and tidy tops, would show up anywhere unprepared, underdressed, without a purse, and with a basket of laundry unfolded. I wondered if the dream suggested she could allow herself to be less formal, perhaps, within the group.

Earlier in the year, I had emailed a poem prompt, "Ironing After Midnight," by Marsha Truman Cooper.

Beth read:

Why does ironing give me such satisfaction? No one can believe I like – even love—to iron. I don't even know anyone who irons. Why do I love ironing? Let me count the ways: It has a beginning and an end, such a feeling of accomplishment! It is a no-brain activity, freeing my no-brain for some of its best daydreaming. It saves money. It is an art form, making patterns on cloth. It is sensually tactile. The hot, hissing steam creates its own mini-sauna, streaming upward to open pores and warm the entire body. The smell of hot fresh linens is ecstasy! Ironing makes order out of chaos, smoothness out of crumples. It gets rid of bumps, malformations, aberrations, and wrinkles.

Ironing is under-rated because of conspiracies by the dry cleaning and medical industries to keep its benefits hidden. You should try ironing—it's cheaper than a psychiatrist, and, moreover, everyone in the household thanks you. It doesn't get any better than that.

"Well, that's it. I'm taking up ironing," Kelly said. Others announced that they would too. Would we someday have an ironing contest? Yes, we would.

We made mind maps, wrote about the vortex in *The Year of Magical Thinking*, and ended the morning with one of our favorite exercises. Each woman got a small folded piece of paper with a different line from the same poem. The line of poetry was her prompt.

The exercise went like this: After our writing period I read the first line of the poem. Whoever got that line read what she had written. We worked through the poem that way, line by line, and at the end I read the poem in its entirety. We all had a much richer experience of the text, knowing what each other had written in response to the various lines.

That morning, I used the poem, "Sweet Darkness" by David Whyte and drew the last piece of folded paper in the bowl.

My line:

Time to go into the dark.

Sigh. I've been there, in the dark. Do I have to go again? Well, night follows day, after all, and the dark is always there. Waiting. But think again. Now I love the night, the darker the better. When Bill stays up late, working in his office downstairs, he complains that the house is so black he can barely find his way to bed.

I don't care if Daphne is lying in front of the bathroom door and I hook her big golden retriever nostril with my pinky toe as I fumble by on my way to the toilet. I could fall and have a terrible accident—broken bones. I've already got the sore knee, the bum hip, the tennis shoulder; that's enough for now.

Still, I love the darkness.

"No," I tell Bill. "I don't want a night light."

As I child I never turned off the lights. A lamp and the nightlight always illuminated my space. I tried to push the dark away but it moved inside me. Even with the house ablaze I often lay in bed alert—sometimes until first light.

Now I say, bring it on. Without a darkened room how can we know those silvery beams of moonlight? Now I wait for the full moon to bathe the bed in its milky coolness.

Now I can sleep with the windows open. I don't worry about the dark climbing in.

Now I say, "Time to go into the dark? Okay. I'll lead the way."

After lunch I offered the prompt. "Write the narrative of your child's death: how it happened, when, what led up to it, what followed."

The women were ready, as a group. They trusted each other, laughed as much as they cried. Nothing shocked them. And they had tools. They could write from different points of view. They could easily incorporate lists, concrete words, clear and original images. They had played with dialogue. They knew the power of verbs. They had written small pieces of the picture, from different viewpoints. They could hear their own voices in their heads and capture them on the page. And they could handle their stories—even think creatively about them. They weren't stuck, the same droning story echoing through their minds. They could now wander down halls and into rooms they wouldn't have entered or even noticed, had they only paced, back and forth, in the same old front parlor.

"There is no right or wrong way to do this," I said. "And remember as with all prompts you don't have to do it at all. But also remember that sometimes it's meaningful to press into what we want to turn away from."

We knew that writing isn't a cure-all, a panacea—there is no cure for grief and trauma—but we also knew that writing offers insight and truth and perspective we wouldn't find if we didn't put pen to paper.

Julie filled twelve pages, front and back, of a large spiral notebook. The words poured out. She had to leave before dinner that night, drive home so that she could lead a church service in the morning. "I tried but couldn't get out of it," she told us. She left her narrative for me to type up.

"I'm gonna do it," Dottye said. She chose to present every excruciating fact head-on.

Man Found Dead

Alex came home from Norfolk, VA on December 18, 1993. He had been out of the Navy since June and hadn't found a decent job and had no reason to stay there.

I was working at a job from Hell, having to leave on Sunday evenings and drive to Union SC (about a three-hour drive). There I stayed in an inn while managing a property under renovation in downtown Union. I came home on Friday evenings. So, I wasn't even able to go to the airport to greet Alex because he arrived on a Thursday and I was in Union.

My son Glenn was living with Walt and me in Westfield, a move he chose as the lesser of two evils, because his dad had moved to Chicago for a job. Glenn had started attending a high school where he knew not one soul and was the outsider.

With that transition, Walt had the burden of taking care of house; animals; a teenage stepson who didn't want to be there; and a wife who hated her job, despised the people she worked for, and spent what little time she had at home crying. Finances were tight, with two daughters (his and mine) in college.

Because we lived way the heck out in the country, I suggested that Alex stay with my mother in town—he'd be closer to job opportunities, good roads, and friends. This has become one of my greatest regrets. If I had known the depth of Alex's depression, and that he was going to be alive only forty-four more days, I would have quit my job, moved back home, and insisted he live in Westfield with us. Another nagging question, "Would that have saved his life?" Also, in retrospect, my mother was too old and had lived alone too long to have a 25-year-old man staying with her indefinitely.

As fate would have it, the weather complicated things even more. It was a terrible winter. There were ice storms weekly, it seemed. For at least a month, the electricity failed every week, meaning we had no water. Walt was struggling to keep kerosene heaters and the woodstoves going so the pipes wouldn't freeze. They did in spite of his efforts.

Then there was Christmas. We have a videotape of the dinner at Grandma's (an annual Christmas Eve tradition) and it is painful to see the despair on Alex's face. Why didn't we see it then?

Alex didn't have any money so I told him I would lend him enough to buy presents for the family. He and Karin and Glenn went to the Mall on Christmas Eve. Karin remembers that evening as the first time the three of them related to each other as adults. It was a special time for her. Alex was 25; she, 21; and Glenn, 16. Glenn also remembers that shopping trip as really fun and "different" from any time they'd had together before. It still terribly pains Karin to remember how bad Alex felt (like a "loser") because he didn't have enough money to buy the things he would have liked in order to "make Christmas nice for Grandma and Mom." He did manage to buy a "funky" watch for me that I still have and treasure as if it were made of diamonds and the purest gold.

The Super Bowl that year was played on Sunday, January 30th — Alex's beloved Dallas Cowboys vs. the Washington Redskins. He went over to a friend's house where all the buddies (and girlfriends of some) gathered for a party. I talked to Alex on the phone on Saturday. He told me about the night before when he and his friends had gone to a country and western music club. He had ridden the electric bull twice. The second time he took a bad spill and his friends had to take him to the emergency room. He had a small fracture, which required a cast and crutches.

But did I ask him about his pain or how he was doing? NO!! I lectured him about how that was going to interfere with his ability to work. He had a temporary job working at a distribution center, moving and stacking boxes. How was he going to do that on crutches? DAMN! DAMN! DAMN! I should have ripped out my tongue. I would do that now if I could. If only I had been a good mother, a sweet mother, and tried to comfort him. If I had understood that he was doing the best he could and was already extremely disappointed in himself and sorry that he had let me down even more. DAMN! I was so STUPID!

That last phone conversation. The last one I would ever have with my son. It gets worse. I also reminded him about the $50 he owed us for the Christmas present money. SHIT! Goddammit!! How could I not know how terribly sad he was already. How could I, his mother, the ONE person in (anyone's) life who should be able to love unconditionally and to be supportive in troubling times . . .

I let him down.

In spite of all that, as Walt reminds me from time to time, the last words Alex said to me were, "I love you, Mom." Walt knows that because he heard me say, just before I hung up, "I love you, too."

In the wee hours of the morning on January 31st, Alex came home to

Grandma's house from the Super Bowl party. Thank God his Cowboys had won and Alex had pocketed his $30 winnings from the betting pool with his friends.

Mother was up early doing laundry and the phone rang about seven (one of her co-workers calling about a meeting later that day). Alex came down about nine and Mother asked if he wanted some bacon. Even though the roads were icy and the temperature still hovered around the mid-20s, as it had for weeks, Alex said no, he was going to try to get out. He did ask, "Was that Mom who called at 7?" How I wish it had been, that I had called and waked him up to tell him I loved him.

As he passed his grandmother on the way out the door, she looked at him with those piercing hazel eyes and said, "Well, when you get back, we need to talk. I'm upset that you came in so late and didn't call to let me know when you were on the way home. The roads are bad and I couldn't sleep because I didn't know if you were going to be all right."

I know Alex felt the piercing and shredding in his heart. I've seen that look from my mother before when she was angry and disappointed in me. And I know how he must have felt. And I am so sad that the last expression my mother saw on Alex's face was one of total defeat. He had disappointed his Grandma and now she was going to have a talk with him.

So he left.

At about six that evening Mother called to ask if I had heard from Alex or if, perhaps, hopefully, he was at our house. I hadn't and he wasn't. I called her a couple of hours later to see if she had any news. She didn't.

Something was wrong, terribly wrong. Alex was not the kind of person who would not come home. I'd had a couple of premonitions in the past month— nothing that I wanted to allow into my consciousness, but they were there . . .

The week before my mother and Alex had come to the house for dinner. I made baked salmon, ham, mashed potatoes and field peas (one of Alex's favorites). It was a wonderful evening. So good, in fact, that I thought, and felt, that everything was going to be okay. Just before Alex and Mother were leaving, he asked if he could take his rifle with him. The boys had had great fun for a couple of weekends with target practice on the land we owned across the road. We walked upstairs together laughing and talking, continuing the mood of the entire evening, and when I reached into the top of the closet and found the gun and handed it to Alex, I felt an unbelievable sickness in the pit of my stomach. I immediately dismissed it as being an overprotective mother—after all, Alex

157

was a grown man; he'd been in the Navy for seven years for God's sake; he'd been bird hunting and target practicing. He knew how to use this gun.

Sometime in the day, I believe in the morning, on January 31, 1994, he did use it.

One last time.

Later that week, a retired police officer who lived in the condos next to Bolton Park would tell how, while taking one of his daily walks, he noticed a car parked there. He heard music playing in the car the first time he saw it on Monday. When it was still parked there on Wednesday afternoon, he went over to investigate. There was no music now. All the doors to the car were locked. There was a young man inside and blood on the seats and windows. It appeared there was a gunshot wound in his head. He called 911.

My nephew, Tom, was en route from his home in Lewisville to Grandma's house to give some continued assistance in our search for Alex on what was now well into the third day he'd been missing. On the radio he heard in a news flash that an unidentified body had been found in a car in Bolton Park. "Man found Dead." He drove to the park, told them who he was — and who Alex was. Tom later took on the gruesome task of recovering Alex's belongings from the car, including the cassette tape that had been playing until the car's battery died, probably long after Alex had died. Tom arranged to have the car cleaned and sold; I never had to see it.

The EMS took Alex to Forsyth Hospital Emergency Department primarily as a place to hold the body until family members could be located and brought in to identify the body.

Tom came on to Grandma's house. We had done the usual things, called all his friends and asked them to call anyone they could think of who might have seen or talked to him. We drove the route he might have taken to work or to friends or to the mall. We called the Missing Persons number in the front of the phone book. We called emergency departments at both hospitals. We called police.

Tom didn't have to tell me Alex was dead. I already knew. I knew on Tuesday afternoon and had already begun to compose the obituary. What would Alex want me to say about him, his life? Should there be any special requests for memorial gifts?

All these things I kept to myself, and waited.

The ED doc put the date of death as February 2nd. He explained he had to do that because they couldn't be sure exactly when he died without doing an autopsy. Over the years it has increasingly annoyed me that the date on Alex's gravestone is wrong. On the other hand, I ask myself why does it really matter? January 31st or February 2nd?

There you have it—the longer version, not the snippet on the news. Man found dead.

Kelly:
Birth and Death
October 23, 2001—The day dawned crisp and cool as they do in the mountains in the fall. I got up excited for my early morning check up.

"Kelly," Dr. Graysinger assured me, "You are fine. You will probably go to your due date (Nov. 13) or even past it." At 36 weeks my cervix was "high and completely closed," the doctor said. "See, I told you. Nothing to worry about."

I left her office with a little bit of dread at having to go four more weeks and a little relief that I had a few more weeks. I had scheduled a picture-sitting for Cameron that morning. We headed out to the Historic Jones House in downtown Boone for the picture, changing him into the adorable corduroy knickers and peter pan shirt. I remember this day in my mind as golden— the vast lawn of this majestic house covered in leaves and the kids (we were with friends) giggling and tossing handfuls up in the air. It is almost surreal— kind of like a movie set.

We then went to a park and Cameron ran until he was exhausted. We hopped into the car for the long ride back to West Jefferson. I really was not feeling well, but I carried the sleeping Cameron into the house and laid him down on our bed, sand and all. Then I settled in for some chocolate ice cream and a good book—I have tried to remember which book but can't. My mom called around two from school. She was having a teacher workday and felt a little worried about me. Suddenly, my water broke with force, soaking the chair and me.

Our sweet baby girl was born at 7:30 that night with the help of my nurse friends, Anne and April, my doula, Lesa, my wonderful husband and even my mother got to be there to see the baby at first sight. The labor was so intensive and quick that the nurses almost had to deliver her. Dr. Marchese called and insisted that he would be in to do a C-section shortly—let's just say they were running down the hall with his scrubs right before the baby crowned. I will never forget him holding her up to me—my only daughter so

159

far and my only vaginal delivery of the four. It took us eight long hours to name her. In the wee hours of the morning we finally decided and hung a big sign on the door for our friends to see—WE FINALLY NAMED HER!!!!! ABIGAIL FAITH SECHRIST, 7lbs 15 oz. 22.5 inches BEAUTIFUL!!! Everyone rushed to the hospital—Mimi and G-daddy, Aunt Heather and Gracie, Gram and Papa…Calls to Germany to Uncle Andy…Aunt Carey from Charlotte.

Earlier, when I held her to my breast for the first time, I noticed some concern and anxiety in the nurses; I thought it was because I was having a post partum hemorrhage. But our daughter was having trouble breathing. Thus began our first adventure with premature babies and their premature lungs. Abigail stayed in the NICU for five of her ten days in the hospital—one night I couldn't stay with her because they discharged me…this was the most torturous night of my life, until a few weeks later. I was pumping every two hours and storing my milk since she could not eat—(fifty-two 4 oz bottles in all). She was on an IV and I begged to nurse her—I just knew that she would get better quickly with mommy milk—besides I was not new to nursing. I had just quit nursing Cameron before getting pregnant with Abby. We watched her oxygen "sats" as we called them go up to the 98 level and fall into the seventies as soon as she came out from under the hood. One day her lung x-rays would be clear, the next hazy. We were so frustrated. Finally she was moved into a room where I could stay with her, only to have to lay her on the "jaundice beach" as we called it, in her eye mask, aka shades. She was under the "bili" lights inside a warmed isolette. I just wanted to hold her.

November 12—Cameron's birthday! We had his party—two years old. Elmo theme, I think? How did I even plan this with Abby only just being born? Everyone wanted to dote over the new baby girl. "She is the spitting image of Cameron," they all said. I remember this party without sound, like the old silent movies. The color is there though, full color. I also remember Cameron's joyful bright eyes. Dimples shining—not one bit shadowed—how this would all change in a matter of weeks.

November 29—Five-week check up with Dr. Neel—Morning. Abby was healthy—well she had a little cold—nothing to worry about—No big deal. She is fine they insisted, healthy enough to have that second HEP B shot. She slept all afternoon.

November 29—Evening. David and Cameron went out to get a surprise for Mommy. They bought a new artificial Christmas tree to replace the shaggy hand-me-down my parents had given us. We put it together—I used one hand, held baby Abby on my shoulder. We got just the tree up, no decorations yet.

November 30—I went to Lisa's house to prepare for the annual Christmas parade—we always did a float with our Moms' group. Babes in Toyland, I think. We took pictures of the kids on the edge of the fireplace—they were smiling. Abby slept.

December 1—Early morning—2 am…Abby would not sleep. I was SO tired. We tried sitting up on the couch. I finally got her to sleep and to her bassinet. She had spit up all over me shortly before I put her down. She was wearing my favorite sleeper hand-me- down from Cameron—white terry cloth— so soft. Around 3 AM she cried out. I put her in the bed with me to nurse and dozed off. At 5 AM she was not breathing. I barely remember screaming for David to wake up. It was absolutely NOT real, still isn't. I kept trying to wiggle or shake her awake. Somehow, I got the phone and called 911—I just kept screaming "MY BABY IS NOT BREATHING! MY BABY IS NOT BREATHING! HELP ME PLEASE HELP ME."

David did CPR on Abby—Trying over and over again to force life into her lungs—I remember the first responder riding up on a four-wheeler—I really would have almost laughed at that if it weren't so awful. Somehow, I called our neighbor, looked up her number in the phone book and asked her to come get Cameron. How did I even do these things? The ambulance finally arrived— they worked and worked on her and finally took her in the ambulance. We followed, at over 80 miles an hour, on country roads. I kept hoping against hope that she would be breathing when we got there. We called my mom and our friends. At some level we knew we needed people there.

December 1—pre dawn. We arrived at the hospital. The physician's assistant and the doctor were with her—Dr. Ingledoo was a young guy—as a matter of fact her son was Cameron's age and had taken swimming with us just weeks before. I just kept staring at her face—mine a mask of terror and grief as they tried just a few last things. TOD—a little after 6…I think I collapsed into David—yelling "NO NO NO!"! Everyone just had that look—the one I came to hate. They put us in a little office to deal with the details. Call the pediatrician. They took her to Ashe Memorial—not Watauga Medical where all our docs were. Call for autopsy. Call our minister. All I wanted was to get out.

The next days are a blur—call the funeral home, write the memorial, find funeral clothes, call friends, family, a steady stream of people and food, someone to tell my grandmother, Mt. Lawn Memorial Gardens...memorials, limo, phone, sleeping pills, being "out there."

We were constantly surrounded for days, weeks even, by family and friends. It seemed like a pit until Tuesday's funeral. My dad, always the minister, went with us to the funeral home. I can't believe I am picking our child's casket, I told myself. This is not happening.

From here on it is just blips of memory—I have amnesia most days. Lists come in handy at times like these.

- *Cameron's stricken little face the day of the funeral.*
- *Sobbing as my dad did the memorial service.*
- *Scott singing "Tears in Heaven."*
- *Up late with Mitzi and Jason the night before the funeral—they stayed over at the house.*
- *Flowers and more flowers. I remember the morning after the funeral. My mom was there at the house. David went into town to the office for a few hours. The living room was dark and damp—damp from all of the flowers and all I could smell was the flower shop. I still hate that smell.*
- *Friends coming from across the state.*
- *The Boone Service League—fed us and fed us in the months following Abby's death—all the way through February.*
- *The people who came home with us after the funeral for dinner—we talked and even laughed some—I think mine was hysteria.*
- *The immediate and pressing questions about Abby's dying 36 hours after her Hep B shot.*
- *Meeting with the doctor—so hard—he was so kind—he has since died of cancer.*
- *The horrible woman from the health department who kept calling that first week, insisting that we "HAD" to meet with her since she was the county SIDS nurse. She was not meant to deal with grieving families—I even suggested that maybe we could get with other SIDS families and she said that we were by*

no means ready for THAT! She also kept referring to the fact that we might be too scared to have another baby! Awful. David and I both left there with a bad feeling.

- *Shopping for Cam's Christmas—in Hickory—we just dragged ourselves around.*
- *The tree trimming gathering that our friends held.*
- *Those horrified looks from everyone who knew us.*
- *I guess there is no ending for this.*

The caged birds in Barbara's living room pecked at their seed and hopped along their perches. Katie Gray gnawed on closed highlight markers before settling down for a nap. Beverly typed for a while then took a break and an afternoon walk. Down the block, she saw and chatted with a group of teenagers she knew who were going to the senior prom that night. Andy would have been one of them. Kathy too ran into some of Ryan's friends.

"Let's not have local weekends anymore," Beverly said. "I prefer getting away from it all. And being so close to the accident site is hard for me."

Kathy agreed. Barbara's house was on the corner of First Street and West End Boulevard. The accident had been farther down on First Street.

An excerpt from Kathy's death narrative:

"Mrs. Shoaf, this is _____ calling from the Emergency Room at Baptist Hospital. There has been an accident and your son is here. We need for you to come right over."

Pause... "What?!"

She repeated exactly what she had said before.

It's funny, the crazy thoughts that go through your head at the most inappropriate times. My first thought was, "Why is Baptist Hospital calling me? Our insurance clearly states that in an emergency we are to go to Forsyth Medical Center..."

"Is this Kathy Shoaf?"

"Yes."

"Your son is here and we need you to come to the emergency room."

"Which son? My two sons are out together."

"Wesley Shoaf is here."

163

"Where is my other son? And where are their two friends?"

"Mrs. Shoaf, all I know is that your son Wesley is here and you need to come RIGHT AWAY."

The urgency in her voice abruptly snapped me out of my foggy confusion and I began to tremble all over . . .

Later that evening at the hospital:

When I finished filling out Wesley's admission papers we (my dear friend had come with me) were ushered into a private room at the end of the hall. The hospital chaplain arrived: very tall, very young, and very nervous. He sat with us in the room that was devoid of conversation and quickly running out of air to breathe. I remember that the chaplain offered us some water, which only irritated me. No, I didn't need any water; I needed to know where my son was! I had no real sense of time, only that it seemed like we waited forever.

Finally, Officer Peterson arrived; male, Caucasian medium height, cropped sandy blonde hair, very business-like. He asked for Mrs. Shoaf. I identified myself and he asked everyone else to leave the room. My friend objected, explaining that my husband was out of town and she was there with me for support. Apparently Officer Peterson saw no need for support or maybe he didn't think I deserved even this common courtesy. He insisted that he needed to talk with me alone. Beverly and Blaine (whom I had called to meet me at the hospital after I received the call), the chaplain and my friend, reluctantly left the room. I was seated on the end of the sofa. Officer Peterson sat in the chair to my left and began to stammer about how these things were never easy.

I had had quite enough beating around the bush. In my desperate need to know the truth I cut him off with, "Just tell me whether my son is dead or alive."

"I'm sorry, Mrs. Shoaf, but your son is dead."

"And what about the other two boys who were with them?"

"They are dead also."

My world spun out of control and I fell to my knees on the floor. The sheer agony and horror of the truth rendered me paralyzed. I was living every parent's worst nightmare. It took every ounce of self-control I could muster to sit back up on the sofa, but I had to hear more. I wanted to know what had happened. I wanted to know where Ryan was. But mostly I wanted him to tell me that it wasn't really true, there had been some terrible mistake, I was dreaming, anything. Just tell me it isn't true.

When I could put words together again I said, "Those two boys' parents are standing out there in that hall. We are friends and they were waiting here with me. Why did you make them leave the room?"

Officer Peterson looked me in the eye and spoke the words that would haunt me for several years to come. "Because you are the mother of the driver. And you are going to have to tell them that their children are dead. And you are going to have to tell your other son too. He doesn't remember the accident and he doesn't know about his brother and his friends."

Judge and jury sat before me in the form of one completely heartless police officer. I had been tried and the verdict was in.

GUILTY.

I'll never know why this officer chose to deliver the news of the boys' deaths in such a cold and cruel manner. Perhaps I was simply the unlucky target of many years of frustration and anger over reckless, teenage drivers. Or maybe he was so distraught at the evening's events that he had to vent to someone and I was the only available person. Or perhaps he truly had no compassion.

I jumped up, jerked open the door, pulled Beverly and Blaine inside and blurted out, "They're dead! They're all dead!" Beverly collapsed to the floor and Blaine and I slowly sank down with her.

"No, no, noooooooo!" Beverly screamed. We sobbed and held one another. I don't know how long we remained that way, but something happened to me in that room. It was as if my spirit separated from my body.

I watched from a distance as Beverly and Blaine suffered and cried. I'm sure that my tears flowed, but I turned off the "React" switch.

Guilt held me in its firm grip. I was the mother of the driver. I didn't deserve to wail and cry for my son. I was somehow responsible for all of this. I needed to step back and allow Beverly and Blaine to be attended to. I was the mother of the driver. My loss was so much smaller than theirs.

Many times that evening I wondered where Ryan was, both body and spirit. No one seemed to want to tell me. I wondered if his spirit was watching me there in that little hospital room, unable to offer explanation or comfort, or if he had already left this earthly realm for his eternal home in heaven. Only later would I learn that it took hours to remove his body from the car. When we said our final goodbye at the funeral home several days later I was somewhat relieved to see that his body was not as badly mangled as my anguished mind had imagined. He was still my handsome, loving son and I could almost hear him say "Don't cry Mama. I will always be with you."

Years later, Kathy wrote again about the night of the accident, in response to a prompt: "Life jackets." She was shocked to realize that her memory of the encounter with Officer Peterson, emblazoned in her head for years, had altered.

Life preservers are instruments of survival. Buoyant objects strapped tightly to our bodies that will keep us afloat, our heads above water, as the force of gravity tries to pull us under the turbulent surface. I discovered recently, quite unexpectedly, that my brain, my soul, my very being had been wearing a life preserver for almost eight years. I've suffered pain, distress and intense anger over the manner in which I was given the news of the boys' deaths on the night of the accident. I've relived that scene in the small, stuffy room of Baptist Hospital over and over and over again:

Police officer Peterson enters the room and asks for Mrs. Shoaf. I identify myself; he asks Beverly, Blaine, my friend, and the chaplain to leave the room. He and I sit at right angles to one another. He begins to stammer,

OFFICER PETERSON: "These things are never easy..."

ME: "Just tell me; are the boys dead or alive?"

OFFICER PETERSON: "I'm sorry Mrs. Shoaf but the boys are dead."

ME: "Those other two boys' parents are standing just outside that door. They were waiting here with me. Why did you make them leave?"

OFFICER PETERSON: "BECAUSE YOU ARE THE MOTHER OF THE DRIVER AND YOU HAVE TO TELL THEM THAT THEIR SONS ARE DEAD."

Those were his words. I should know. I was there and the scene has replayed in my head until my memory was exhausted. I cried to my counselor about it. I complained to our lawyer about it. I even went to see the Chief of Police after Wesley's legal proceedings were finished and I knew that there would be no repercussions for my son.

But then, on a cold morning, the third week of January, 2010, I awoke with the realization that my memory was wrong. This is what was actually said:

ME: "Those other two boys' parents are standing just outside that door. They were waiting here with me. Why did you make them leave?"

OFFICER PETERSON: "Because you are the mother of the driver." Period.

That was all he said.

I realized that he did not say: AND YOU HAVE TO TELL THEM THAT THEIR SONS ARE DEAD."

No, he didn't say that. Here's how the conversation continued:

ME: "Don't we have to tell them?"

OFFICER PETERSON: nods

ME: "Now?"

OFFICER PETERSON: "Yes."

Then I jumped up, jerked open the door and delivered the news that would alter our lives forever.

OH. MY. GOD! WHAT? How can this be? I was sure that my memory had been correct. I was horrified, embarrassed, and incredulous. I was also certain that the memory I awoke with that morning was accurate.

Why would I have remembered it incorrectly for all those years? I was too ashamed to tell anyone until I talked with Bryan, my counselor, a few weeks later. He explained that this was not uncommon. In times of intense trauma, our brains often skew the facts. It's a protective measure; a way to conceal the parts of the story that we are not ready to handle.

My guilt was self-imposed.

For eight years I've not been ready to let go of my responsibility for this whole tragic event. I'm ready now. I was the best mother I knew how to be. Nothing I could have done could have changed the awful events of March 29, 2002. So now, I'm letting go of the guilt. I'm taking off my life preserver. I know that now I can swim.

As the afternoon wore on, we gathered on Barbara's sweeping front porch, taking turns with Katie Gray, watching the shadows stretch longer and chatting quietly. Some of the women were still in the house working.

For the first time ever, we took the entire evening off. No prompts. No writing.

On Sunday morning we drank coffee and ate pastries in Barbara's dining room before getting started.

We wrote about how a typical day in our lives might start. This can be a good exercise in list-making and in cultivating awareness—what do we think about, how do we proceed through our days, how might we shift what we do a bit? I had seen a prompt somewhere: pretend you've been given a day off from your life. Someone is stepping in to be you. What does this person need to know about you, your idiosyncrasies: Do you stumble into the kitchen to feed the cats first thing? Does your husband bring you coffee in bed? What happens?

After what had been stirred up the day before, I wanted to offer something simple and fun—a new look at the mundane, the quotidian.

Kathy's piece was punctuated by a school-morning refrain—"Time to get up, Mandy."

Barbara's poem:

Routine
Awaken to the alarm
 darn those singers!
Hi Bud – I love you too.
Coffee, shower, make-up, pills
 hand me a towel with a kiss.
Should I walk or drive today?
 newspaper says rain
Damn! Someone's in my parking spot
 how dare they?
Walking in with the masses
 do I use this time clock or the one across the way?
Mary Jane's at her desk.
Judy's brought more flowers.
Fumble with my keys.
Computer screen quiet… waiting…
 one message from the "Marshall family"
 still hard to think of my daughter that way
 a few more emails
 what's new at the medical center?
 check the home account
 something funny from Beth
 where does she get these things?
 seven spam messages – shit!
 check my school account
 Why hasn't that grade been posted yet?
Time to get to work… check the patient list.

168

Awww… she died last night

>*hope it was peaceful*
>
>*hope her daughter was there*
>
>*hope that particular nurse was on duty*
>
>*will have to find out the details later.*

Send the list around.

Pager goes off

>*"Sure, we can see him today – tell me a bit more."*
>
>*Oh, hi Morgan (I'm learning to tolerate you better.)*
>
>*Oh, God, why did you do that?*
>
>*Maybe I'm not so tolerant after all.*

Uh, oh. It's gonna be one of those days! Which pager is that?

>*"Why of course – we'd love to talk with her family. What have they*

been told so far?"

>*(I'm sure not enough!)*

White coat is on now

>*load my pockets*
>
>*walk a bit straighter*
>
>*smile at folks in the elevator*
>
>*oh, my, she must have someone really sick in here*
>
>*"Sure, I can help you find the ICU"*
>
>*"Hope your day gets better"*

Another page?

>*"Oh, Bud, is it lunch time already?"*
>
>*"No, I can't go now."*
>
>*"You can't go in an hour?"*
>
>*"Give me a call later."*

"Hi Jackie! What's it gonna be today?"

>*"Pork loin?"*
>
>*"Black-eyed peas?"*
>
>*"We'll take the chicken."*

"What time are you going to be finished today?"

>*"Yes, I love you… I'll do the meeting. Keep your tennis time."*

"Can we please go to bed early tonight?"

>*I'm beat.*
>
>*What a day.*
>
>*"Let's cuddle."*

HOPE

It was only four o'clock on Friday afternoon and Dottye was popping champagne bottles in the living room of Scharme's beach house. Beverly and baby Hope had just arrived; we would finally be meeting "our" (we already felt possessive of her) adopted girl from China. High fives, kisses, the clink of glasses. Loud voices—huge milestone: Katie Gray and Hope and all of us, together.

Scharme kept her promise to have us back, even though she had fallen and broken her hip.

"There was no way I wasn't going to have you all this year," she said, leaning on the back of a chair. "I need my sisters."

She was using a temporary walker and couldn't put any weight on her right leg. Somebody remarked it was a weekend of strollers and walkers.

Our only laments were that Julie and Kathy couldn't come. Julie was facing breast cancer surgery—we offered up several moments of silence for her over the weekend. Kathy had made a big lasagna and was all set to join us, but her grandmother died the night before our get together. She had to stay home for the funeral but sent along the dish. "Eat some for me," she'd said.

Because so much happened on our retreats, we always regretted when anybody missed one. The writing could be typed up and shared. The unfolding of the time together couldn't be. We made awful black humor jokes and collected anecdotes that became standard lines within the group. We shared so many moments that would never, could never, be repeated.

My younger daughter Colette (in the photo) came along for the weekend to babysit for Hope and Katie Gray so that we'd be able to get some writing done. (Katie was fourteen months, Hope, eleven.)

"Wow, Mom," Colette told me. "I knew you loved to party but I didn't know the others did too."

"This is unusual," I said. "It's so special for us to finally be able to celebrate Hope—in person."

The wait for Hope had gone on for over two years. At last, in July, Beverly and Blaine had been told they could go to China to bring their little girl home. And here we were, meeting her in September.

From China Beverly had written five long emails. This excerpt was written when they'd had Hope for just a few days:

Hope "talks" and laughs around us constantly but is a bit quieter when we are out in public. I think she's still trying to figure out this whole new world. Think about it: she lay in a wood-bottomed, steel-barred crib for nine months; she had probably never had her ears cleaned out; she had never tasted pear juice or Cheerios or strained prunes...okay, she still doesn't like those. Mostly though, she never had two doting people talk to her and play with her and hold her close...two people to love her with the hearts of parents.

When she was handed to us not only did her clothes reek of urine, but her little feet were filthy too. I kissed her feet because she needed them to be kissed. I bathed her after we got back to our hotel room and the washcloth was dirty. Yang Xi Lu Lu's world has changed. She is now Hope Lu Burton. Blaine's world and mine have changed. We are now a family again. We love kissing her feet. It doesn't matter if they are dirty or clean. She is our daughter.

Hope rested on Beverly's hip, her shiny-black, chin-length hair clipped in a pink barrette. She had round cheeks, filled out since the photos Beverly had sent from China. Her dark eyes attentive, she was taking it all in—one face at a time. She reached her little arms out to us as we greeted her, then turned her body into Beverly's shoulder, overcome by momentary shyness. Who wouldn't be a bit awed, with all these women cooing and pressing so close? Before long we were passing Hope around, kissing the top of her head.

Finally, Hope was here.

I recalled an overnight trip Beverly and I had taken to visit Kelly earlier that year, when Hope was still a faraway dream, only a hope. Kelly had let us all know that winters were dark and cold and hard for her, living in the mountains. Her husband David, a self-employed Information Technology specialist, worked on office systems, often on weekends when they weren't in use. Kelly spent a lot of time alone with her three young children and she welcomed company. We would be grown-up entertainment, friends who would drink coffee with her, help her fold laundry, distract her children. Kelly had written about her situation:

Family Matters

We are who we are as a family, as David, Kelly, Cameron, Cohen, and Katie Gray because of our other daughter and sister—Abigail. Our family does not exist without her or outside of her, and we remember her as though she inhales and exhales every breath with us. We traveled to hell and back over the past seven years—much of that because of our grief and some of it in spite of it.

Life goes on and other bad things happen and the greatness of life continues in the same unending cycle. Our marriage and relationships have suffered and bounced between clinging tightly to each other and completely turning our backs on each other. We have walked, driven, and run blindly through tears. We have prayed with fervor and cursed a cruel God. We have watched baby monitors and sweated through spinal taps on our babies.

We almost lost another child to a septic infection in his blood stream and spent weeks on bed rest with our fourth child. I suffered dark depression and anxiety and finally saw a glimmer again. Just because we have light now does not mean that our love and grief for a daughter lost is gone—it only means that

172

On Saturday morning, I read aloud another poem "Choosing a [sto]ne" and sent the women out to the beach to choose stones. [The]y all came back saying, "Hey, teacher, there are no stones on [the] beach."

["]Sorry," Monica said, shrugging, "Can't write without a stone."

["Go] get a bucket of sand and write about that," I told her. "Sand [was] stones once upon a time, you know."

[I]t was a rowdy time, unlike any other so far. We had become as [com]fy as old sweats in each other's company. But there was a cloud [over] the weekend: Julie's cancer and surgery. She was facing her [own] mortality up close and personal.

["Being sick myself isn't as hard as losing Jack," Julie told us. ["Lo]sing my boobs? No comparison."

it intensifies. David and I both, along with our children, have found ways to deal with our losses—we run, we go to church, we revel in the magical things of our world and for now we pay homage to the empty chair at our table.

Beverly had been looking forward, "Well sort of," she said, to changing Katie Gray's diapers—more practice for the day when the baby would be Hope. "Remember. I never had a girl to change."

The February day was gray and damp as we zigzagged up the two-lane road, around precipitous curves and mountain drop-offs, to Kelly's house outside Boone, North Carolina.

"She needs to move away from this road before her boys are old enough to drive," Beverly said. "It's treacherous."

"No kidding."

As we pulled into Kelly's driveway on that wintry afternoon, my cell phone rang. It was Colette.

"I better take this," I told Beverly. "She doesn't usually call in the afternoon, and when she knows I'm with any of you guys."

"Mom, I can't believe what happened last night." I heard the wavering in her voice, the struggle to keep back tears. I glanced over at Beverly, who was looking right into my eyes with her deep blue ones.

"What happened?" I asked.

"Two boys were rough-housing at Andrew's dorm and they crashed through a window and fell three floors. One of them is dead, the R.A. for the floor."

"Oh Colette, I'm so sorry."

Beverly's forehead wrinkled. "Is everything okay?"

I told her quickly what happened. The color drained from her face, turning it chalky. Young men rough-housing. She knew all about it. The irony of this call coming at this moment was not lost on either of us.

"I'll go on in," she said. She reached over and squeezed my shoulder.

"I'll be there soon."

I watched Beverly get out of the car, close the door, and walk towards Kelly's house, her back straight. Without this group, the three of us, Kelly, Beverly and I, would never be getting together for an overnight. Kelly, young, with small children, led a busy life campaigning for her dad, a Democrat seeking a State Senate seat. Beverly, her orderly house now empty of children, offered Bible study to young women from her church. And me? My kids were grown; I was decidedly secular; I spent most of my time leading workshops, coaching writers, and visiting my elderly parents a flight away. How would our paths have even crossed?

The curled-under mountain laurel leaves rustled in the wind. A wan sun peeked out from behind a bed of clouds, then retreated.

When I got off the phone, I rushed up the path to the front door, too engrossed in what Colette had just told me to notice the area off to my right, the Abby memorial stone with three angels, one for each of Kelly's other children.

"Tell me everything," Beverly said. "I bet I know some of those boys in that dorm." She and Blaine had kept up with all of Andy and Wes's friends as they grew and went off to college. Wes would probably, she told us, have headed to NC State to study engineering or computer science. The Burtons also hosted an annual golf tournament in memory of Andy and saw a lot of his friends through that.

"I'll say a prayer for those families," Beverly said, shaking her head. "Me too," said Kelly.

By now, both women knew that I don't exactly pray. "I'll be thinking of them all," I said.

We're an odd combination of women in this group. Kelly, Julie, and I are life-long Democrats, sloppy housekeepers, Liberals. Beverly and several others come from more conservative traditions: spotless homes, probably Republican, though we've never discussed our political affiliations officially. Beverly is a devout Christian and enjoys Christian rock. Once she had told me that, though I wasn't religious, she did sense I was spiritual.

The visit with Kelly had brought it all back to Beverly—two boys about two years apart, tumbling like puppies all over the floor, getting sent to their individual bean bag chairs to calm down, and vying for Beverly's attention. Beverly was a child magnet and it's no wonder. She was a vibrant blonde with an expressive face, and she worked as a professional storyteller, though she'd barely told a tale since her boys died.

BACK TO ROARING GAP

We opened our second Roaring Gap weekend with a poem, "Why I Need the Birds," by Lisel Mueller. "Why I need..." I said. "What do you need? Let's write."

Dottye called out: "Why I need 'American Idol.'"

"Okay," I said. "Write about why you need American Idol."

That weekend we realized how much everyone's writing had changed, expanded, lightened. I passed out random photos as prompts. Julie (pictured above) wrote fiction about an elderly man in a hotel lobby; Kathy wrote from the point of view of the toys being played with by a boy in the photo ("I, the Legos . . ."). Peggy created a fictional piece about the unspoken secrets of two young women in sunglasses.

A discussion followed about the book you're reading now. Where we were with it? The women in the group ragged me, saying we'd all be dead by the time the book finally came out. I told them they'd had fair warning: I'm a slow manuscript producer. Monica said, "We need another grief writing contest. If people send enough writings in maybe we can guilt-trip Carol into working on the book!"

We had actually held our first "Grief Contest" on a Saturday morning in 2005. I had challenged everyone to type up her workshop writings and send them in to me between 10 a.m. and noon. The person who sent in the most would win.

At ten o'clock that Saturday, the emails started appearing in my in box. I copied them into each woman's individual folder. Monica was determined to win.

Strive for Five
Strive for 5 is my plan
To get ahead of the rest of the clan
Word after word I type away
Then off to Carol to file today

Email from Me: 10 Minutes Left
Dear All:
OK. If it were word count I think Julie would win but since it's number of submissions Monica wins—with eleven. Some are short (questionable) poems she composed today.

Julie, you need to send two more to recapture the lead. No nail-biting now. It's only, as Beth's husband Sandy would say, a grief-writing contest.

My final email: 12:01 PM
It's now after twelve. The contest is officially over—no more submissions accepted.
Monica won.

Here we were, once again, on a glorious weekend retreat at Roaring Gap. We were holding an edit session so that everybody could work on what they had written. Many of these women hadn't seen themselves as writers when we started but we had become a writing group; we were no longer just a grief-writing group. I asked them to notice how their writing had changed over the years.

We observed that when we wrote about "a place that no longer is," for example, I was the only one to write about my dead child, how his baby room had morphed into a bedroom addition after my husband and I no longer owned the house. Others wrote about all sorts of places: a childhood kitchen, a grandmother's front yard tree, an elementary school, and "being marched under cold showers at a summer home." Often our writings included references to our losses but certainly not always.

We weren't sure what form the book would take but I had asked them to select and organize some of their favorite writing into a chapter. I talked about some of the obvious challenges we all struggle with as writers: omitting needless words, cutting adverbs, showing not telling, using active voice and action verbs, choosing the concrete over the abstract, and watching out for cliches.

"Are we back in high school?" Kathy asked. "I'm not sure I can do this."

"Don't worry," I said. "These are just things to think about, not when we're actually writing, but later, when we're revising."

I began to sense that editing wasn't the right activity for the afternoon. Some of the women had closed their books, squirmed in their chairs for a while, and were sitting on the back patio enjoying the mountain view. Others hovered over their pages, looking grim and worried.

I told them to relax, that we'd have another session at a later weekend. "At this rate we'll never get a book done," Beth said. "We'll have to leave the task to you, Kelly, our youngest member."

"Like I have time!" Kelly said. "Me, the mother of three little ones!"

"Books go through many phases," I said, "and take a lot more time than we think."

"We'll get there," I said. "Imagine if we had tried to write this after one year of meeting, as some of you wanted. We've needed all this time to learn about what we are as a group and what we've become."

The memoir I wrote about my son who died in 1982, hadn't been published until 2001. I ruminated for years before the words began to tumble onto the page. When they did, they came in torrents.

But more years would pass before I could finally wrangle the sprawling story into a book. I'm quick at banging out newspaper columns, buying houses, and chopping garlic. For the most part, I edit other people's manuscripts in a timely manner. I plan and lead ongoing writing workshops and travel the world offering others. But when it comes to my own books, I am the tortoise. Three other manuscripts are collecting dust on the runway behind this one, hoping the fuel won't run out before takeoff.

I was struggling to find a way to bring all the components together into a single book. I was always telling my students: Let the content dictate the form, but I was a bit stuck. At one point the book was going to contain a chapter of short pieces by each woman. A companion volume, by me, would discuss our writing process and the group.

As some smart person somewhere said, we teach what we need to learn.

After our edit session, I suggested we take a silent walk to clear our heads, to observe and listen and keep our mouths closed for a change. We would write about our impressions on our return. It was a crisp day. We started out in silence, with people stopping to observe, as we ambled along the old logging trail, the fields of tall grasses and shade trees and the empty milkweed casings. Before long, laughter erupted, and the chatter started. People whispered, "Shhh, Carol wants us to be quiet."

I felt like a camp counselor.

"I know I have no authority over any of you," I said finally. "Go ahead, shout it out!"

By the end of the walk everybody was talking.

"It was a good idea though," Kay said "just not with us, apparently."

Sandy took us on boat rides around the Roaring Gap lake. He puffed cigarette after cigarette as he steered and told us about the surrounding land. I sat directly downwind of the smoke with Julie across from me. Better for me to breathe the smoke—she was recovering from breast cancer surgery.

Julie: *Eye Contact, Please*

I have maybe twelve minutes until the kids get off the school bus. I will use them to do not morning pages, but afternoon. Hell of a morning. The mammogram showed a spot on my left breast, then they did another mammogram, then an ultrasound, and there is something there. The doctor's first choice was to jump to early stage breast cancer. Shouldn't they teach them to say what it could be instead, first?

Also, shouldn't they teach the doctors to look at and talk to the patient, and not the husband? I was so annoyed, and I could tell Dan was too. He wouldn't look at the radiologist, but was looking at me, trying to redirect the doc to talk to me. It helped a little.

God, I hate those little rooms. Nothing good has ever happened to me in those little rooms. Someday I am going to write about those little waiting rooms. Little NICU rooms. ICU rooms. ER rooms, in hospitals in different cities in North Carolina, in Chicago. Doctor's office waiting rooms. Rooms where I am the patient, the sister, the mother. It doesn't matter, it all just goes to hell in those little rooms. It sucks to be sitting there alone, staring at the posters on the wall, or leafing through the magazines, trying not to think about what the tests are showing and why the hell is it taking the doctor so damn long to get back in the room? Oh my god there must be something really wrong. And it sucks when the room is crowded with family, because I've done that too. Eight or ten of us jammed into one little NICU family room where they tell you that your family will not, after all, be continuing to celebrate the addition of another family member. Where you shift into extended family mode and start wondering about how your mother-in-law feels about you and why is your sister crying over there? Who asked her to come anyway?

And god I hate it when my dad cries. And doesn't the doctor hate doing this? No wonder he says his piece and leaves as fast as he can. And why is it so hot in here, or is that because I just had surgery and the pain meds are wearing off? Do I have cancer? Do I really have to wait two weeks to find out? Can I please just not sit in one of those little rooms again when they tell me?

Since we'd been meeting, some of us had lost parents, in-laws, aspects of our own health. Peggy had had two heart attacks and now Julie, the second youngest in the group, was dealing with cancer. Three of us had critically ill husbands. Dottye's sister was mentally ill and homeless, living on the streets of Las Vegas; Beverly's older sister had developed early dementia. We tracked each other's lives and offered our support. Some of the women who lived close enough got together for coffee. We all understood that one loss brings up all the others. We could be there for each other, knowing more than many friends and family, what losing means to a bereaved mother.

The writer Anna Quindlen has said, "We are defined by who we have lost." In an article entitled, 'Grief, more than Death, Renders us Silent," she wrote (about her nieces, whose 40-year-old mother had just died), "My brother and I know too much about their future; both teenagers when our mother died, we know that if the girls were to ask us, 'When does it stop hurting?' we would have to answer, in all candor, "If it ever does, we will let you know.'"

She goes on to say, "The landscapes of all our lives become as full of craters as the surface of the moon. I write my obituaries (for the *New York Times*) and think about how little the facts suffice, not only to describe the dead but also to tell what they will mean to the living all the rest of our lives."

We ate out that night at a local family restaurant that specialized in fried fish and served nothing harder than sweet tea. We had to sit at a long table, shared with others, strangers—not the best venue for us. Instinctively, we perceived a truth about our particular group: we were drawn to hunkering down in a house together, preparing our own meals, or at least bringing in ready-made food. We needed the continuity of being together without having to put on public faces and head out into the larger world. People can always dine out together; they can't sit and write together all day, take a break for tea and a meal around a table together, and then get right back to it. Many of us were happy to stay all weekend in our yoga pants.

GRIEF WRITING CAMP

By the time I arrived at Emerald Isle, Monica and Peggy were already there, making and coloring pictures. They had put a little handmade paper sign in front of a red plastic bowl:

"ART for SALE: Please help send us to Grief Writing Camp."

"There's art by the locals for sale down at the gas station," Monica said. "Why can't we sell there too? We need money for grief camp!"

Somebody had put two pennies in their bowl. As people arrived they gravitated to the table and ended up drawing. Beth copied a sea bird and a shell.

"She's good," Monica said.

Even Dottye, once she got her bra off (the first thing she did to announce that she was going to relax), sat down and created a picture, well, sort of a picture. A child's scribbling better describes what covered her page.

"Do we have to write this weekend?" Peggy asked. "Let's just make art."

Somebody always resisted; it was a standing joke with us now.

"Writing is so hard," they would say, only half kidding.

True. Sometimes sitting down to write seems as bad as sitting in a dentist's chair, mouth open to prying sharp instruments. But unlike the dentist chair, once we settled down and began, we felt inspired, even swept away by the voices and images rising up and claiming space on the page. After writing, we felt more open space inside us, more room to breathe.

"Our first prompt segues well from this art work," I said, once everybody had arrived. "It's an ambush prompt with pictures."

An ambush prompt, so named by a student from another workshop, was a prompt you couldn't choose. It chose you.

Groans around the room.

Pick one from each bowl," I said. In one bowl, face down were newspaper headlines: "All I ask for is a little respect," was one. The other bowl held recent newspaper photos—a young woman curled up in the back of a truck, a female athlete sprinting. "You can keep these, paste them into your journals."

"We really are getting arts and craftsy," Scharme said.

"Not really," Dottye said. "Carol's just getting more and more wacked."

"Here's what else you can do," I said, ignoring, as always, the gentle jibes. "Keep a bowl at home with photos, quotes, words, whatever and pick one or two as ambush prompts for yourselves. And keep adding fresh material to your bowls."

"Sounds fascinating," Monica said, in her monotone.

I knew that no one would probably set up a bowl at home. Often the women didn't write in their journals at all between sessions. The room was quiet again for the writing.

Kelly and Beverly had left their toddlers at home this year. "There is no way anybody would get anything done if Katie Gray were here this year," Kelly had told us. "She is into everything."

After writing and reading, it was time, they insisted, for more arts and crafts. Beth had brought a Christmas holiday project—to decorate with red ribbon the little beeswax candles in holders that she had made for all of us.

"These are a Moravian tradition," she said.

"Can I at least have a little wine with the arts project?" Dottye asked.

She uncorked a bottle. We got out snacks, and hovered around the dining room table, making a red frill for the candles or drawing and painting—except that is for the slouchers (they will remain nameless) who sat on the couch doing Sudoku puzzles.

We relished our usual fresh shrimp seafood dinner, sitting out back, the waterway breeze cooling the evening air. Scharme waited on everybody, the intrepid yet relaxed hostess. Her hip tissue was regenerating, her prognosis good. She was healing, finally, and walking well.

After dinner, Barbara told us about her stint in South Africa, as part of her nurse practitioner training. She had been haunted by the smell of death on the children she visited. She would hold a dying baby and wonder what good her gesture did, in the face of all the death and disease surrounding her. She told us how horrified she had been at the poverty and corruption all around her.

When she finished, I said, "Let's all get out our journals and write about what we've just heard. The smell of death. Barbara's words."

Whenever someone reads or discusses a difficult subject in our group, we write in response. We always do this. We did it when we first met and when we got the fabulous news that Beverly was adopting. We are a writing group. Writers are people that write.

Later that night, Dottye showed a clip of her son doing stand-up comedy and a longer piece about her visit to her homeless sister in Las Vegas. Beverly showed videos of Hope. A group played the game Balderdash, where each player makes up a definition for an esoteric word. I didn't want to play, but as I listened I realized what wordsmiths and word lovers this group held. And I also realized we were always going to be a group, always going to get together to write, share, and play, maybe not always twice a year but, still, always.

On Saturday afternoon we had another editing session. I told people to read over everything they had written since the formation of the group and write a response to what they'd just read. Authors Louise DeSalvo and James Pennebaker say that writing about traumatic matters can relieve distress by encouraging healing shifts in perspective. The writer gets the words down on the page and then says: "Oh, I hadn't seen it that way before." Or, "I can revise my thinking now."

It's a privilege to be able to revisit earlier writing, especially in the company of trusted companions. I thought back to when I wrote the memoir about Malcolm. All those journals I had scrawled—they felt like the work of an obsessed court reporter. I thought at the time that by writing I had released, somehow shed, the experience. Not true. Yes, the observed world lived somewhere else, on the page. But it was through rereading and finding a meaningful narrative—all those years later sitting alone at my kitchen table in the predawn hours—that I actually began to heal.

A lovely quiet settled over the house, the peace you feel when a baby is napping. I told them this was rare: we had time to edit our writing individually, yet still be part of a group. Peggy disappeared to work on her grief narrative, announcing. "I am going to finish it this weekend." Everyone read and wrote and edited. Some of the women commented on how much, over the years, their feelings had changed, their perceptions lightened, and their writing loosened up. A few asked me questions about grammar or talked about other aspects of writing.

We focused for hours, well, most of us. A few took walks or swims. Monica and Beth talked about heading down to the gas station to try to sell their drawings.

Eventually, we gathered to respond in writing to a Gina Kolata piece from *The New York Times*, about female runners who get faster as they age.

"What gets better with age?" I asked.

"Can we write about this group?" somebody asked.

"Of course," I said. "Has a subject ever been taboo?"

I have never gone to a high school or college reunion. I doubt I ever will. With a few exceptions, the people I want to keep up with are my friends and connections from later years. Like Barbara, I am not particularly a joiner though I seem to be part of or a leader of many groups. I have offered many one-day writing workshops for bereaved mothers but so far I've found I can only be a fully-participating member of one, this one. This is my group; these are my people.

Way back when Malcolm died, I shared hospital time with a woman whose elegant teenage daughter Lydia suddenly swelled up and lay on the brink of death, after what should have been a minor heart repair.

Lydia's mom said to me, "You know, Carol. There are groups for people in our situation."

I shook my head. "Not for me."

I was not ready for a group; couldn't even imagine being in a group. But that was a long time ago. After more than twenty years, I have created and now lead the group I would have wanted to join back then, if I hadn't felt half-feral and unfit for human company.

I looked around at this group of women, heads bowed, words spilling out onto their pages or tapping out on their keyboards. We have all surprised ourselves with our writing, even me the group leader.

At a summer writing residency I had given for a different group, not long before our beach retreat, I wrote a piece that startled me. One of the many things I love about writing with others is that, like everybody else, I too will have insights into my own heart and work. I'll hear my own voice percolating on the page and I'll be as vulnerable as the next writer. What comes up will be new, even though I may have written to the prompt many times before.

I gave a Pat Schneider prompt, "In this one, (referring to a remembered photograph) you are . . ."

"It may be a photograph of you" I said, "or from a dusty family album your grandfather put together when he returned from the Philippines after WWII. Pick a photograph from your memory."

An image flickered across my mind and my stomach tightened. "First thought," I told myself, referring to the poet Allen Ginsberg's imperative to write about the first thought, in this case the first photo that pops into your mind. He said it will be the best idea. I always tell this to groups.

But I ignored my own advice and started writing about second thought, a familiar photograph: me standing head-on to the camera, a tow-headed toddler, in a cotton sunsuit, with Michelin-tire-man sturdy legs. In my outstretched hand I'm holding a large fish over a bucket. Crouching to one side are my two older sisters in profile, squinting in the sun, their short hair clipped back in barrettes; they are watching me, noses wrinkled, squeamish. Mother has her arm around me and is smiling at the camera in her 1950s stylish white-framed sunglasses.

Familiar territory. I've written about this picture many times. I realized as I wrote that I was bored with the story. Me, the baby of the family, "Carol the Barrel," being brave and silly and chubby. This might go somewhere interesting, I told myself. Keep writing.

No, another voice in my head said. Go back.

That first image, the color Polaroid, splashed again across my inner screen. In this picture I see my husband Bill, in green scrubs. A blue facemask hangs like a bandana around his neck. He's got his arms around our just-born-by-cesarean first child, Malcolm, and is holding him out in front of his chest, not quite sure yet how to nuzzle his freshly-born boy. Why this picture, I wonder? I've written about other Malcolm pictures, though there aren't many from his short life.

But I needed to follow this lead. It was beckoning to me. I'm always telling everybody else to follow their forceful images. I love this about writing. Images bubble up, seemingly out of nowhere, and begin to flow, like a brook over stones—scenes that wouldn't have presented themselves had we not been in the act of writing.

I wrote from Malcolm's point of view, the way I have other people do, the way Barbara did about her son William and Kathy about Wes:

In this Polaroid you are holding me. You, Daddy, in green scrubs, your curly hair already graying at the temples, balding on top. I am fresh from the waters of your wife's womb, I, your first born, your only son. I am going to rip you up, blast a hole through your heart, leave you in shreds, like my mitral valve leaflets; they're tattered. Nobody but me knows this, yet.

They had to cut me out of her because I knew that once I was born, breathing on my own, the trouble with my heart would start and never stop. Hold me while you can. I won't be here long.

In the poem "The Guest House," the poet Rumi says to open yourself to

188

everyone who comes into your life, all the visitors, and that's what I am, a brief visitor:

> *"Welcome and entertain them all!*
> *Even if they're a crowd of sorrows,*
> *who violently sweep your house*
> *empty of its furniture..."*

I am going to do that to you, Daddy.

> *"Be grateful for whoever comes," Rumi continues,*
> *"because each has been sent*
> *as a guide from beyond."*

This is a writing prompt you give often, Mom, this Rumi poem. I, your flesh and blood, am a guide from beyond. If I could speak I might say to you right here, right now in this hospital operating room, to you Dad in your scrubs:

Take me home to die.

Don't rush me by ambulance this Saturday morning to one hospital, then another; don't tear me down the middle twice and tamper with my willowy heart. Don't stick me in the head with needles, the only place anybody can find a good vein. Nothing can be done, ultimately, to save me.

Let me go home with you, meet my puppy Molly, curl up with you two on the green couch. And die.

I would say this but you're not ready, not able to hear it. And what parent is? Take me home to die? No way, kid. You must do what you're going to do with me. In time you will learn not to fear death, even the death of babies, but you don't know that here, in this Polaroid.

I am a guide from beyond, and I am the worst and the best thing that will ever happen to you.

I often skip reading aloud altogether if we're pressed for time or word-saturated. If I do read, it's almost always at the end, after all the others. Everyone else had read at this summer program in a North Carolina college. It was my turn. But I didn't want to end the entire residency with this piece of painful personal writing that had shocked even me.

I'll save this, I told myself, to share with my grief writing camp. They will understand.

Over dinner that night at Scharme's beach place, we talked about our first meeting, more than five years earlier, and how surprised we all would have been if, say, Diane Spaugh had told us, "In five years you'll be at Emerald Isle, and there will be two new little girl babies, and you'll plan on meeting regularly until you can't anymore."

"It just shows," Peggy said, "that you never know what's in store. So don't give up hope or think that the way you are now is the way you're always going to be. It's so hard with grief, to have any distance."

Dottye read us a fund-raising letter about an effort to name her daughter Karin's classroom after Alex. Karin was a middle school Spanish teacher.

"Karin learned so much from Alex," Dottye told us. "Things came easily to Karin but not to her brother, and she has always been drawn to the child in the room who's having the most difficult time."

Over the years, many of us have offered legacies in honor of our children—special book sales, March of Dimes walks, art donations to hospitals, scholarships in our children's names, honorary sports events, and even building funds.

We all love this story, from Barbara:

The Ball

For years after William's death, I was haunted by the yearning to tell his story. I felt that there had to be a legacy. I toyed with the ideas of races in his honor, annual fundraising events, and the like. This need to tell his story stayed with me for years. And at the same time, I was haunted by another fact, that I hadn't stood up at his funeral and given him a standing ovation. I knew he was deserving, yet I sat quietly in my seat. I have regretted that moment for years.

At the ten-year anniversary of his death, we learned of a Make-a-Wish event called the "Celebration of Hope." Hope Stout was a young girl who, before she died, was given the opportunity for a "wish" through the Make-A-Wish Foundation, a wish-granting organization for children with life-limiting illnesses. When asked what her wish would be, she astounded everyone by saying that her wish was for all the children on the waiting list to have their wishes granted. A fundraising gala was held and the necessary million dollars was raised to grant Hope's wish. Her parents decided that this should be an annual event. We learned of this event and decided this would be the year to "give the ball back."

William Goldsmith was a budding basketball giant when at the age of seven, he was diagnosed with neuroblastoma, a form of pediatric cancer. He was already showing promise of being a basketball star, although he still needed a little height. He loved basketball and he REALLY loved Michael Jordan. Therefore, it came as no surprise when he was offered a Make-a-Wish trip that he would want to meet the all-time best basketball player ever.

When we arrived in Cleveland, where the All-Star game was being held, the city was alive with excitement. 1997 was a special year for basketball because it was the 50th anniversary of the NBA and was therefore designated as the year to celebrate the fifty greatest players of all time. Loads of events were planned for the players and for William—from the private players celebration to the rookies game, the 3-point shoot out, the slam dunk contest and of course, front row seats at the All-Star game.

William was getting autographs from lots of stars. But the highlight, of course, was Michael Jordan. Because of security, only one parent could accompany William to actually meet Michael. It was never a contest. Bud would accompany him! About forty players passed by, some acknowledging William, and some barely glancing his way. Then, like the hero William imagined he'd be, Michael Jordan came down the corridor and greeted William. Michael was incredibly gracious, taking time to shake hands, have a picture taken, ask William where he was from and talk about how he LOVED North Carolina. Michael made sure to warn William not to yell too loud at the game because "that might make me nervous."

William practically floated back to his Mom, speechless, cancer the last thing from his mind.

All of the signatures carry their own stories. And to this day, this ball has never been allowed to touch the ground.

So on the 10th anniversary of William's Make-a-Wish trip and death, and the year he would have graduated from high school, we knew what to do. William had said, up until the end, that meeting Michael Jordan was the best day of his life. Months after his trip, while he was dying, he would have what we called "morphine dreams." He would be talking to all the people who signed his ball and he would be smiling. Make-a-Wish made his last days bearable.

We always believed that the ball belonged to Make-A-Wish. We knew this was the year to "give it back." We really wanted it to bring BIG money, and we *knew it was worth a lot, but much of its worth seemed personal. So we put a $3000 reserve on it—if it didn't earn that we would bring it back home—sell it another way and give the money to Make-A-Wish.*

Well, they wanted us to stand up there and walk the ball around during the auction, while they read the letter we wrote. Of course we were all tears. The auctioneer started it at $10,000 but didn't get a bite, so he lowered it to $5,000 and that was where it started. Some of the sports enthusiasts in the audience bid it up from there, $1000 at a time. There was a lull around $12,000, but then it took off again. When it got to $17,000, the auctioneer said, "going once, going twice..." and sold it. A standing ovation followed.

The buyer announced that he wanted to give the ball back to the parents. Suddenly there was some commotion and someone came up and told the auctioneer that if that meant the ball was back for sale again, there was a buyer for $25,000 — so it sold AGAIN!! Another standing ovation.

Unbelievably, once again, it was announced that the ball was being given back to us.

A few other things we learned—when the $17,000 buyer wrote his check at the end of the night, he "rounded it up" to $25,000 as well—so this ball brought $50,000 for Make-a-Wish AND we brought it back home.

We were about as blown away as we could be . . .William finally received the standing ovation (twice) we always regretted not giving him at his memorial service.

For us, this event was somewhat of a closure. It took ten years to find the right way to honor him, to tell his story and create a legacy. I guess my advice to parents who are searching for such an opportunity would be to not give up. The right time will come when you can honor your child in the way he or she deserves. Even if it's ten years later.

Beth wrote about how she and Sandy had wanted to donate a piece of art to one of the hospitals where Branner was treated. She and I visited the hospital on one of my trips to Winston-Salem and saw the magnificent piece of artwork the Baldwins commissioned.

Beth:
Butterflies
"In the bulb there is a flower; in the seed, an apple tree;
in cocoons, a hidden promise: butterflies will soon be free!

In the cold and snow of winter there's a spring that waits to be,
Unrevealed until its season, something God alone can see."

I love that piece of music, called the "Hymn of Promise." Every time I hear it, it makes me cry inside. They always sing it at funerals of beloved children killed in tragic accidents or of a young wife struck down by cancer in the prime of life. I thought about having it at my own son's memorial service, but knew it would be my total undoing and quickly decided against it.

I especially like the part about the butterflies. I often ponder my personal beliefs about being born into new life. Is death like a cushy cocoon that releases gossamer souls to a new glory? I'd like to think so; it certainly seems like a prospect I'd love to embrace.

One thing's for sure, there's SOMETHING about butterflies. At Bran's grave that day, there was a single yellow butterfly flitting all around during the whole service. Everyone in our family saw it and commented on it. There was a lot of comfort in that butterfly.

When it came time to choose a piece of art in Branner's memory for the new Regional Cancer Center, we thought long and hard about an appropriate message. There are many stunning landscapes and paintings of nature that would speak to Bran's love of the out-of-doors. However, nothing we considered seemed quite "him." And we certainly wanted something uplifting for the Cancer Center.

Then, we saw it. Sandy and I were vacationing on the island of St. Martin. We decided to stop by a butterfly farm one afternoon on the way to dinner in Philipsburg. There on the wall of the tiny gift shop were iridescent butterflies of all sizes and colors, preserved in mid-flight and encased in acrylic.

We were able to locate the butterfly artist in New York. We both became teary-eyed when we saw the work he created for us and for Branner. He called it "Into the Light." It's a fan of huge blue and white butterflies, soaring to the heavens. In one corner of the panel, a small yellow butterfly spreads its wings and takes flight. We trust that these colorful and majestic butterflies bring joy and hope to the many cancer patients and their families who pass by each day on their way to seeking a cure.

"Butterflies are among the most gorgeous of creatures, noted for their glorious colours.

Their wings are emblazoned with the evidence of their ancestry,
like the quarterings on the shields of ancient nobles."
That's the inscription beside the butterfly art.

If we were to assign a mascot to our group it would be a butterfly—not a possum! When I was working on this book in a mountain cabin, a monarch rested on the porch rail beside me and spent most of the week fluttering around me, even following me on walks.

We've all had meaningful encounters with butterflies. Beverly wrote this piece about butterflies and faith:

In August of 2001 (almost seven months before Wes and Andy died), I was weeding my flower garden and Wes was fiddling with his jeep, his pride-and-joy. A blue and black winged butterfly flew up to one of my flower stalks and I noticed that it was hardly able to fly—torn and tattered from a hard summer, probably a near-miss with a bird. I watched it make its way to several flowers, then I called Wes over. I told him something like this: "Wes, look at this pitiful butterfly. It can hardly fly and yet it's still doing its job, gathering nectar. Its wings have taken a beating this summer. But, it's still doing what God created it to do."

Then I said, "You know Wes, life can be like that. You will go through lots of stuff that will beat you down and tear you up inside, but you can still go on, if you draw your strength from the right source—God. He will give you what you need to keep going and doing what He created you to do."

It wasn't too long after Wes and Andy died that I remembered telling Wes all that. It's so ironic that Blaine and I are living that lesson, not Wes and Andy. Butterflies have become an important source of inspiration for me.

I love flowers and when we moved to our new home less than nine months after the accident, I had to create a flower garden. We had a perennial garden at our other house and I wanted to take my flowers with me—Wes and Andy knew how much I loved my flowers. It was early June before I was able to transplant them from their holding pots to my new bed in our new yard. I had been digging for less than 10 minutes when 2 yellow swallowtail butterflies found their way to me. They lighted less than a yard from me, side-by-side. They were not torn and tattered like the one almost 2 years earlier. I watched them and decided that Blaine needed to see them too. He was mowing the front yard and I went around and yelled for him to stop and come see them. They continued to flutter around our backyard and periodically light near me, always side-by-side, for about an hour.

Blaine and I wish that we could go back to March 29 and change what happened at 10:10 p.m., change the course of history. Life doesn't give us that opportunity, but God does give us the opportunity to live a life to honor Wes and Andy's memory and to glorify Him. Blaine and I try to do that. And God keeps sending us butterflies. He keeps giving us hope.

In the epilogue to Dottye's piece about Alex's suicide "Man Found Dead," she writes about the car in which he had killed himself and what happened with the money from the sale:

Alex's Car Money
The car was sold for $700.
Walt had the idea, when none of us could decide what to do with the money, that Grandma, Karin, and I take a trip. We went to Louisville, KY on our first "Triple G" (three generations) trip together. We went to the horse races at Churchill Downs. We have continued this 3-G tradition and take a trip of some kind, somewhere, annually even if it has to be a day trip due to health or other considerations. We have learned a lot about each other and about ourselves. It has been a gift of honor, intimacy, and love.

This introduction of horse racing, and our mutual love of gambling, has evolved into another deeply valued family tradition. That is: every year Walt and I and ALL the kids, significant others, and grandkids go to Lexington KY to visit Keeneland Race Track and other sites of interest there and along the way. . . .

When Malcolm died we set up a memorial fund in pediatric cardiac surgery at Boston Children's Hospital in his name. Dozens of people donated; we never knew how much money but the director of development sent us several letters; each updated us with the names of those who had recently given to the fund. Those letters and the people who gave money were extremely meaningful to us. I could hope that someday some other baby wouldn't have to suffer as Malcolm had in his short life.

I will always remember my little boy's rage. Even though he was only six weeks old, I sensed he was furious when that first open heart surgery repair failed and his pink chubby body began to turn pale and blue again. We were on our way out of intensive care, so hopeful and excited.

Wait. This can't be happening. We're packed and ready to go; we're taking our healthy son home. But it was happening. The patches sewn so meticulously onto his mitral valve leaflets failed to contain and control the flow of his blood the way they were supposed to. He kicked and fumed as the color drained out of him and a thin line of sweat appeared again on his upper lip. He fought me when I tried to hold him. I sensed he knew he was a goner. I could not comfort him.

Over the years after he died, I realized I was no longer afraid of death or of anybody's stories about death and illness and suffering. In fact, I wanted to do penance for all the times, the times before Malcolm—when I was young and scared—that I had turned away from people who were grieving and in need. Twenty years after my son died I offered the first full-day writing workshop for bereaved mothers.

Each workshop I give now, any kind of workshop, I give in my boy's honor, my son who never had a chance to speak or write or develop his own quirky style. It is my hope that through writing others will be able to tell their stories in their own voices, feeling apologetic to no one, getting at the truth, and letting that guide their words on the page.

Sunday morning at Emerald Isle was another perfect day. Some of us walked before breakfast.

Monica:
Ghost Crab
Walking the beach early this morning with Kay, I had a thought as I viewed the various sunken footprints parallel to the tide lines. Some prints were of the human sole; others were manufactured soles with various print configurations.

On occasion, a ghost crab hole appeared in the sand—quarter-sized, leading nowhere or to some dark and narrow musty place away from civilization. Around the hole stood small heaps of sand from within, shooting out in all directions, as if something had dug desperately to get away from this above-ground world.

Suddenly a wee little ghost crab appeared, running feverishly sideways, its color blending into the freckles in the sand.

Early on after Katie's death, I saw myself as the hole, dark and deep. In time and with the help of this group, I became the ghost crab making an occasional appearance, trying to blend in, even if moving in a different direction from my feet. Now I see myself as the firm footprints in the sand, walking with renewed strength and determination, as far as the path takes me.

Around noon our ritual packing up began. We stood at the kitchen island, eating sandwiches and divvying up the food. Always so much leftover food.

"Who wants these two packages of perfectly good rolls?" Kelly asked. "And these bagels."

"Who wants some slices of this chocolate cake?"

We started loads of laundry for Scharme, tidied up the bathrooms, and crammed our cars. Another weekend together. Before we all left, I gave two to-go writing prompts:

• Walk out the door of your house without a plan and let possibilities introduce themselves.

• Welcome the chance encounter.

We continue to meet twice a year, sometimes more frequently. Kay now has five grandchildren. Monica and Barbara each have three. Peggy's son John, Kathy's son Wesley, and my daughters, Olivia and Colette, are married. Kathy's daughter Mandy graduated from college with honors. The hospitality house (SECU Family House) Beth and Sandy worked tirelessly to get funded has opened and is serving dozens of families; Dottye is the Manager of Educational Services. Julie's family has bought their first home; Kelly's has moved to a sunny house at the beach. Scharme feels healthier than she has in a long time. Betsy's son got a PhD in history. He and his wife have a new baby. Beverly's Hope, "Hope Lu Burton," is thriving. We support each other in times of difficulty.

Knowing when and where to end this story is hard since we keep writing and keep getting to know and enjoy each other more. To celebrate our tenth anniversary we're planning a trip to a chateau in France, for a week of writing, reflection, good food and wine, and, of course (with this group) fun. A few of the women are applying for passports for the first time. I've taken groups of writers to this chateau for a number of summers, but it's especially fitting to take this group. Everyone has come so far since we first met. We are all, indeed, farther along.

We decided to close with Julie's response to a line from a Mary Oliver poem, "When I Am Among the Trees," from our September 2007 weekend at Emerald Isle beach. Here's the line Julie drew from the bowl: "But walk slowly, and bow often"

Julie:

But walk slowly, and bow often to the waves hiding schools of fish that dart across the crest.

Bow to the wind that blows sand across my ankles, stinging them.

Bow to the path for the sea turtle hatchlings, ready to bear them across the dangerous sand.

Bow to the pricklers gathered on the rug inside the door, a threshold to hold the pain.

Bow to the counter where food piles up, where we stand and drink wine and eat shared bits of our other lives.

Bow to the women in this room, writing ourselves whole.

Walk slowly on these weekends, and bow often.

So, we all say to you, in closing, walk slowly and bow often. And, of course, write.

Epilogue: Weymouth Walk

Go on out and take yourself for a walk. It will blow the stink off ya.
—Irish wisdom

When I was working on this book, I spent a few days at a retreat center in Southern Pines, North Carolina, to try to make order out of all the Word documents I'd collected since our first writing workshop and to move the project forward. I found myself struggling, a not uncommon state of mind for me when I'm writing:

In spite of the December sun sparkling off the magnolia leaves, I am beginning to sink into gray. Fog rolls inside my head. Where am I going? All these words, files, drafts strewn around the room. I only have these few days to work on my own writing—this book—before returning home to my over-stuffed life as writing teacher, editor, coach, wife, daughter, homekeeper, and mother.

I pull on my coat and head down the gravel drive of this estate to the barn. I find comfort in the dark walls, in the smell of leather and hay and manure. I like to listen to the horses chew, their huge yellow teeth crunching—steady, muted, like a meditation.

A stocky older man in a felt cowboy hat, jeans, and riding boots stands outside the barn. He is smoking a pipe. The back of his jacket is emblazoned with the initials "USA" and an American flag.

I remember seeing this guy and several other men when I stopped in yesterday on another of my avoid-the-desk missions. They sat in a half-circle just inside the open double doors, smoking, chatting and drinking coffee. These are the guys who care for the horses, hitch them up to buggies, feed and groom them. I made small talk yesterday, careful to deflect questions about where I was from or what I was doing. I didn't want to talk about myself. I teased them about what I called their "men's group."

"This is the only time we can get together," one guy with a big red nose said, "you know, before working."

"When are you getting your drums out?" I asked, "for your drumming circle."

They laughed.

"Men have things to talk about too, you know," a tall lanky man with bad teeth volunteered.

"Want a cup of coffee?" another asked.

"No thanks," I said. "I'll just take a quick look around."

They joked about women showing up. "Out of nowhere," somebody said, "comes a broad." They laughed some more. As I walked through the barn, though, they grew quiet.

"Don't let me keep you from talking," I said, realizing just how awkward my presence probably was for these guys.

"Hell all we talk about is Viagra and stuff like that," the skinny guy quipped.

"Well then," I said. "I'm out of here, for sure."

More innocent banter. I thanked them for letting me look around and stepped outside.

This morning as I approach the stocky man doesn't let me off so easy.

"Where are you from?" he asks, in an Irish brogue. His sharp blue eyes drill straight into mine. He is determined to know.

"I'm from Chapel Hill," I say, "Staying up at Weymouth, to write." I nod toward the mansion.

"Ah and what you writin' about?" he asks.

Why had I offered that? Why do I open my mouth and let my brains fly out? Why hadn't I just told him I was taking a walk to admire the shrubbery? People walk these grounds every day. Why do I always give more information than necessary? As my daughters are always saying, "Too much information Mom; that person doesn't care."

"I'm working on a book about a group of bereaved mothers," I blurt out. "I've been meeting and writing with them for several years."

"Ah," he says. "Tough stuff. No wonder you're down here at the barn, not writing."

"Yeah," I say, brightening. Somebody understands—a total stranger in a USA jacket.

"I lost a son ten years ago," he says, piercing me again with those blue eyes. "He was twenty-four years old. Died in February and was set to be married in July."

"I'm so sorry," I say. "I lost a son too, in infancy."

He tells me about his son's death, how he died in his sleep from an irregularity, a narrowing, in his esophagus. He choked on his own vomit.

"The same thing happened to his first cousin three years later," the man says, "and he didn't even drink. It's, you know, a genetic thing."

I can tell this detail, "it's a genetic thing," is something he feels he must add to his story to ward off the "was your son drunk?" inquiries, as though now that he's dead that matters. All of the women in our group know the pain and shame of dealing with questions and suppositions from those who haven't lost a child.

He squints up at a tree then looks down and kicks at the ground, the way a horse might. He tells me that his wife went out of her mind for five years, but "now she has found religion and that helps her." Listening to his stone-cold tone, I can tell religion hasn't helped him and that he and his wife are estranged in their grief. Don't ask me how I know this. You just do, after a while.

Another man appears at the barn door. My stocky fellow bereaved parent shoots him a quick glance before saying to me, "It's been good talking with you. Hey, write that book of yours. It will help people."

He turns and walks into the barn.

It is our group's deepest hope that this book will help people, especially those who have lost children.

PROMPTS AND RESOURCES

Here are the prompts from each of our writing get-togethers.

DAY ONE:
All-Day Workshop
(first meeting)

1. As an opening exercise, write about a safe place, a healing place, using as many senses as you can. How does the air feel, smell? What do you see? Hear? Smell?

2. Just the Facts. Have each woman write her child's name, date of birth and death, and the cause of death. Go around the room and have everyone read what they've written, only what they've written.

3. Written Reflection: After everyone has read, invite them to write again, about what they have just heard from the others in the group.

4. Sentence Stems help warm people up. Choose the writing subjects appropriate for the group: I am a person who . . .As I child I spent a lot of time. . .I was encouraged to. . . I first encountered death when . . . My family believed . . .Something I can't talk to others about. When people ask how many children I have, I say . . .

5. Make lists. Lists are easy, quick, and can be used later to jog the memory as ways to promote further writing. Make a list of fears and worries, regrets, things I miss most about my child. I ended with: "Make a list of what you're grateful for."

6. Write about this: How Many Children Do You Have?

7. Draw a line down the whiteboard or a large piece of paper.

Write "before" on the left of the line, "after" on the right. Invite the participants to call out words that correspond. What was my life like before the death of my child? On the right, What was my life like after the death of my child? This exercise not only elicits feelings that get put into words, it also builds a sense of community, of shared experience.

8. Pick a word from each list and create an acrostic poem. That's when you use the letters of a word as a starting line. If "love" were the word, the first word of the first line would start with an "L," the second with an "O," and so on. There is no limit on how long each poem line has to be.

9. Have a dialogue with an aspect of self. I often read an example from a student: A dialogue with procrastination, love, insomnia, or self-consciousness. Use warm up prompts to help writers find an inner quality with which to dialogue: When I'm self critical I tell myself. . . When I'm feeling wise I notice . . . Whose voices do I hear in my head? My mother's, my older sister's? What kinds of things do they say to me? Pick an emotion or situation that's forefront in your mind and a word that goes with it. Dialogue with that word.

10. Write about something that belonged to your child.

11. Set out a collection of art prints, some dark, others bright. Use abstract (Georgia O'Keeffe for example) and realistic. Tell writers to pick a print that appeals to them and write about it. Describe it and see where that takes you. Make up a story about an aspect of the print. Write from the point of view of someone in the print. Let a story emerge.

12. The unsent letter. Write a letter to your child.

13. Invite your child to write you back.

14. Write about what stands out from this workshop. What do you want to write about that you didn't have time for? What advice can you give yourself right now?

15. When you get home write in response to a poem. Try William Stafford's poem, "Yes." William Stafford lost a child.

16. Make a plan to write again. Write down your plan.

CAROUSEL CENTER
Half-Day Session (second meeting)

1. Read over what's in your journal and write about what you find, notice.

2. Write about being among this group of women again. How do you feel?

3. Write about something particular you remember about your child: a habit, a gesture.

4. Read aloud "Snowdrops," the poem from Louise Gluck's collection, *The Wild Iris*. Use any line from the poem as a starting prompt. Consider writing from the point of view of something in nature—a tree or flower or stone.

5. Write about yourself in the third person. "She . . ."

6. In closing, write about what brings you peace.

BREATH OF SOL
Weekend (third meeting)

1. Do a body check and write about where you're holding tension.

2. What matters? I added some other ideas to this theme: What's going on? What's different now since we met last time? I also invited the women to reread what they had written about their sanctuary, their healing place, from the first session.

3. Write about your expectations. What are your hopes for this weekend? What do you especially want to write about, work on, do, while you're here? What are your goals for this group? How do you feel now, one year after the group first met?

4. Dialogue with a body part. Start with sentence stems. For each, write your answer on the page:

A part of my body I'm happy with . . .

A part I don't particularly like . . .

When I'm upset my body feels . . .

Where in my body do I hold grief, sadness? How does it feel?

When I'm relaxed my body . . .

When I want to do something nice for my body I . . .

Pick a part of your body that's calling to you and have a dialogue with it, the way we had with an aspect of self at our first meeting. Set it up as though it were dialogue from a play:

I tell the women to give the body part the last word. Ask it at the end if it has anything else to say. (These voices rarely get to speak and when they do, I warn the women, they can be sassy, demanding but also informative, truthful.)

5. Make a list of self-care activities. Write in detail about one of them.

6. Write about something you've done, an unusual activity, since your child died. Before responding to this prompt, we read and discussed Raymond Carver's story "A Small Good Thing." The father of the dead boy in the story cradles his son's bicycle wheel.

7. Take a walk in the woods and write from the point of view of something in nature. I read "Stone," a poem by Charles Simic.

8. I read a Robert Frost poem, "Never Again Would Birds' Song Be the Same," written after his adult daughter died. Through bird calls, he kept her close; she lived in their song. Prompt: How do we stay close to our children? What in the natural world reminds us of them? Why? How? What else reminds us?

9. Write about the items you've brought for our memory shrine.

10. Write about rituals in your life.

11. Write a short tribute to your child based on how you feel today.

12. Make a gratitude list.

OVERNIGHT
One-Night Retreat (fourth meeting)

1. What's going on in your world right now?

2. Cluster or mind map. Put your name or an emotion you're struggling with or a topic of interest or concern to you in the middle of an unlined sheet of paper. Circle it. Let ideas come to you about the word. Draw lines out from the central word and write an idea. Circle that. Let an idea come from that idea. Make a line out and circle the next idea. You end up with a spider web of linked ideas. Take one encircled idea and write about it in detail.

3. Respond to the poem, "Imperfection," by Barbara Carlson. *"The way I never get the sink really clean, lose my car in parking lots, miss appointments I have written down…"*

4. What do I carry? Read excerpt from Tim O Brien's novel, *The Things They Carried.*

5. Write about "never and forever." (Beth's suggestion)

ROARING GAP
Weekend (fifth meeting)

1. I remember…

2. Respond to: "I Used to Be But Now I Am," a poem by Ted Berrigan.

3. Write from the point of view of one of your surviving children.

4. Write in response to the essay, "Joyas Voladoras," about hearts, by Brian Doyle (from *The American Scholar*).

5. Make a self-care list. Pick something from it and write about it in detail. Write about a self-care item of somebody else's that you'd like to incorporate into your life.

6. Write about visions of the dead: Kay suggested a prompt from a book we'd read: *Eva Moves the Furniture,* by Margot Livesey: "She needed neither speech nor gesture to get my attention; her presence thickened the air, as if light bent slightly around her."

7. Write about your picture. (I had asked each woman to bring a picture of herself as a little girl.)

8. Write about gifts that you have and use. From *Swimming Lessons*, a memoir by Penelope Niven. Not all of our book selections were about grief and dying. This was about learning to swim as an adult and about life lessons: Gifts you have and don't use. Write about how you could start using them. I like to end our weekends with something useful, something we can take away and from which we can draw strength.

YOGA
Day Session (sixth meeting)

1. Write deeply about something important that has happened to you since you were last with the group.

2. Respond to: "Talking to Grief," a poem by Denise Levertov. Where are you now in relationship to grief? What does grief look like, feel like? What metaphors or similes would you use to describe grief—as a dog you won't let into the house, as in the poem?

3. After doing an unusual activity together (taking a yoga class, for example) write about the experience.

4. Write about "The Country Beneath the Earth," a Margaret Atwood poem. What does it mean to descend and return?

5. Write about forgiveness. Have you ever forgiven anybody? Not been able to forgive? Asked to be forgiven? What does forgiveness mean to you?

6. In closing, I gave a series of short reflective prompts and asked the women to answer the same questions from the point of view of childhood, the present and five years in the future:

A word that describes my childhood . . .

As a child I liked to . . .

I needed to . . .

I spent a lot of time . . .

I was expected to . . .

I hoped to . . .

A word that describes my life now . . .

I like to . . .

I need to . . . (etc.)

Five years from now a word that will describe my life is . . .

EMERALD ISLE
Weekend (seventh meeting)

1. Write a short autobiography, five minutes, and include one lie in it. The group will try to pick out the lie, so make it good. (I first wrote to this prompt in a workshop offered by Pat Schneider. It's

an excellent ice-breaker for a group and helps writers focus on the difference between fiction and non-fiction.)

2. Let a shell or something on the beach find you. Write about it.

3. Write about a personal failure and what you learned from it (Beth's idea)

4. Write to this: "I Am From . . ." based on the poem "Where I'm From" by George Ella Lyon.

5. Prompt: 13 Ways of looking at a Beach (I read them my poem, "13 Ways of Looking at a Fountain"—based on the Wallace Stevens poem, "13 Ways of Looking at a Blackbird.")

THE DEATH NARRATIVES
Weekend (eighth meeting)

1. Give out a piece of paper with a large blank circle on it, a mandala. Color it in with what grief looks like and tell or write a story about the coloring.

2. "What's inside?"

3. Record a dream and write about what it might mean.

4. Read Joan Didion's *The Year of Magical Thinking*, before the weekend. Write about the grief vortex.

5. Cut a poem up into lines and hand them out. Write in response to your line. Have someone read the poem, stopping at the end of each line to hear what has been written about that line. Then read the poem all the way through, by itself.

6. Write your death narrative. Take all afternoon if you need it.

7. Make a list about the morning. What do you do? How do you start your day? Write in list form, if that suits you.

HOPE
Weekend (ninth meeting)

1. Read the poem, "Choosing a Stone," and invite the participants to walk the beach collecting stones and then write about what they find.

2. Cut up lines from "Grandmother Speaks of the Old Country." Write about a line from the poem.

3. Write about other mother figures you have known, based on Sue Monk Kidd's novel, *The Secret Life of Bees* (the Black Madonna).

4. Write about your mother's body, based on an essay by Mary Gordon.

5. Read "Psalm," by Stuart Kestenbaum. Write about spirituality.

BACK TO ROARING GAP
Weekend (tenth meeting)

1. Write about this: Why I Need . . . based on "Why I Need the Birds," a poem by Lisel Mueller.

2. Respond to a random photograph.

3. Write about silence.

4. Read over and edit some of your favorite writings.

5. What do you breathe in, breathe out?

6. Write about a place that no longer is. (based on a poem called "Drucker's Mule Barn" by Jeffrey Franklin.)

7. Make a collage page using photos, lines from your writings, anything else you want.

8. Write about the poem, "Optimism," by Jane Hirshfield.

9. Consider resilience. Write.

GRIEF WRITING CAMP
Weekend (eleventh meeting)

1. Choose a random headline and picture. Create a story. Hand out newspaper and magazine pictures glued to colored construction paper—a Third World woman standing with a group of straggly children as soldiers walked by, an emaciated fashion model in a tattered slip, a family at breakfast, an elegant older man reading a newspaper in what looks like a leather-furnished book lined hotel lobby. Hand them out one, face down. Turn over your paper and respond to your picture.

2. Write about your gremlin. First I read an excerpt from a book *Taming Your Gremlin* by Rick Carson, in which he talks about this nasty little creature we all live with, whose goal "from moment to moment, day to day, is to squelch the natural, vibrant you within."

3. Write about your line from the Mary Oliver poem, "When I Am Among the Trees."

4. Edit session. Read over your journals and write, revise, daydream on the page.

5. What gets better with age?

6. Respond to Naomi Shihab Nye's poem, "The Art of Disappearing." How do you disappear?

7. Write about what you see as your child's legacy now.

8. I read a quote from the Vietnamese Buddhist monk, Thich Nhat Han, which begins "Every morning, you rededicate yourself to your path . ." and ends "Don't compare yourself with others. Just look to yourself to see whether you are going in the direction you cherish." Write about going in the direction you cherish.

RESOURCES

There are so many excellent books and writers. Here are a few of our favorites.

BOOKS ON WRITING:

Writing Alone and With Others, by Pat Schneider

Reading Like a Writer: A Guide For People Who Love Books And For Those Who Want to Read Them, by Francine Prose

Writing as a Way of Healing, by Louise DeSalvo

The Art of the Personal Essay, edited by Phillip Lopate

The New Diary, by Tristine Rainer

Writing to Heal, by James Pennebaker

A Broken Heart Still Beats: When Your Child Dies, by Anne McCracken and Mary Semel

True Nature: An Illustrated Journal of Four Seasons in Solitude, by Barbara Bash

NOVELS:
The Things They Carried, by Tim O'Brien
Eva Moves the Furniture by Margot Livesey
The Secret Life of Bees, by Sue Monk Kidd

MEMOIR:
Blue Nights, by Joan Didion
The Year of Magical Thinking, by Joan Didion
Circling my Mother, A Memoir, by Mary Gordon
The Best Day, The Worst Day: Life with Jane Kenyon, by Donald Hall
Comfort, by Ann Hood
Hours of Lead, Hours of Gold, by Anne Morrow Lindbergh
Gift From the Sea, by Anne Morrow Lindbergh
Swimming Lessons: Life Lessons from the Pool, by Penelope Niven

POETS:
Barbara Carlson, Billy Collins, Louise Gluck, Jane Kenyon,
Maxine Kumin, Denise Levertov, Ted Kooser, Lisel Mueller,
Mary Oliver, David Whyte, and David Wagoner.

ONLINE:
The Writer's Almanac: http://writersalmanac.publicradio.org/
Poetry Daily: http://www.poems.com
The American Scholar, the print periodical and the site: http://
    theamericanscholar.org
Our Blog: http://writingtowardwholeness.wordpress.com

I Want to Help

At one of our weekends we made lists of gestures of kindness and consideration that had really mattered to us, shortly after our children died.

There's a big difference between those who can just "be" with the bereaved as witnesses, without judgment, without trying to fix what's unfixable, and those who thrive on being in the center of chaos and tragedy. If you want to get involved with a grieving family, approach with kindness and without an agenda. Be willing to sit, listen, and be present. Leave your fixed ideas and your nosy-neighbor self at home.

Here are some suggestions—from lists we made—that worked well for some of us:

• As we planned the funeral, we found songs that each of us wanted included. We gave this list to a friend who put together a CD of music to be played at the funeral service.

• Get a volunteer to provide sheets of paper to funeral attendees, with the following questions: Your name_____, How you knew _____, Stories about _____. For months Beverly and Blaine received long letters from former teachers, coaches, and many of their sons' friends, telling stories about the boys, things they never would have known.

• If you happen to be at the accident scene or witness the death in a hospital or wherever, write to or somehow talk to the family, letting them know you were there. One of the first people who stopped at the crash site when Elizabeth died waited in line for hours to speak to Kay at the funeral home visitation, even though she hadn't known the family.

• If you are a nurse or a doctor involved in caring for the dead, show up at the funeral. Or at least send notes to the family. The on-duty nurse who helped deliver Abby came to her funeral. A young intern who lived across the street from the Burton-Shoaf accident was the first person on the scene. He sent notes to both families, and continued to write, for several years, at Christmas. He provided particular comfort in letting them know there was nothing anyone could have done to save the boys. They died instantly, as did Elizabeth Windsor.

• Little gestures can be monumental. Call and ask if the bereaved person wants to go for a walk. Peggy appreciated those friends who continued to make themselves available to her even when she wasn't able to return phone calls or accept invitations. (She felt so unlike the social person she had been before Rebecca died.) She still feels grateful for those who took her out for walks and simply listened to her.

• Beth talked about people who came by and took out the garbage, who helped build a ramp up to the front door, who brought food, and who did laundry.

• One friend stayed at Dottye's house for three days around the time of the funeral, fielding phone calls.

• An English teacher in whose class Elizabeth Windsor might have been had she lived, collected poetry responses from students a year after her death (with the writers' permission) and sent them to the family. All of the writings contained some connection to Elizabeth and their remembrances of her.

• It's never too late. The deputy who came to the door and told Kay's family about Elizabeth's death wrote them almost 15 years later, saying that Elizabeth's death and delivering the news to them had changed the direction of his life. It had been the first time he had ever had to do such a thing, as a young deputy. The experience caused him to alter his path in law enforcement; he took courses in crisis management and victim assistance, and that became his life work.

ACKNOWLEDGMENTS

Without the support of Salem College for Women, Home Moravian Church, and Hospice of Winston Salem, the first workshop would not have happened. Special thanks go to JoAnn Davis and Diane Spaugh at Hospice: the organization gave me a start-up grant for the book. I'd also like to thank Claire Christopher, Jim Sparrell, Margy Campion, Carolyn Karpinos, Katryna Hadley, Susan Kennedy, and my husband Bill Henderson. Two week-long stays at the Owl's Nest cottage at the Wildacres Retreat Center in the North Carolina mountains provided a divine place to write. Weymouth Center for the Arts and Humanities in Southern Pines, NC offered another writing refuge. I am utterly grateful to each woman in the group for being willing to show up, dig deep, and share her writing. I can not imagine my life without these splendid women in it. I don't know what I would have done without Kay Windsor who tirelessly edited text, worked on photos, and always speaks in a calm voice. Kay also set up and maintains our blog, with Monica Sleap. Thanks so much.

CPSIA information can be obtained at www.ICGtesting.com
Printed in the USA
BVOW012344190812

298195BV00002B/2/P